C000231165

JAMES L.

The Millionth

The Story of the R.101

Published by
James Leasor Ltd
81 Dovercourt Road, London SE22 8UW

www.jamesleasor.com

ISBN 978-1-908291-20-2

First published 1957
This edition published 2015

for
MY FATHER
who served in the RNAS
during the First World War

'I do not see any other difficulties that prevail against this invention save one, which seems to me the greatest of them all, and that is that God would never surely allow such a machine to be successful since it would create many disturbances in the civil and political governments of mankind. Where is the man that can fail to see that no city would be proof against surprise when the ship could at any time be steered over squares, or even over the courtyards of dwelling houses, and brought to earth for the landing of its crew? Iron weights could be hurled to wreck ships at sea, or they could be set on fire by fireballs and bombs; nor ships alone, but houses, fortresses and cities could thus be destroyed with the certainty that the Airship could come to no harm, as the missiles could be hurled from a vast height.

FRANCESCO LANA, *on the Aerial Ship,* 1670.

'She is as safe as a house - except for the millionth chance.' LORD THOMSON OF CARDINGTON, *on the Airship R. 101,* 1930.

ACKNOWLEDGEMENTS

I would like to acknowledge the very great help that many people have given to me. In particular I owe a heavy debt of gratitude to the following:

Mr J H R Allen, Mr Percy Atkins, Wing Commander and Mrs Ralph Booth, Mr J W S Brancker, Sir James Barnes, Mr Harry Bateman, Mrs A G Bransom, Mr John H Binks, Mr A V Bell, Mrs L Bradley, Mr Leonard Burman, Sir Harold Roxbee Cox, Mrs Eve Waley Cohen (formerly Mrs N G Atherstone), Wing-Commander T R Cave-Brown-Cave, Miss Laetitia Chitty, Mr J H Collingwood, Mr T S D Collins, Mr J H W Cope, Mr H C Dickin, Air Chief Marshal Lord Dowding, Mrs Doris Everard, Mrs P M Ford, Mr and Mrs J Fordham, Mr and Mrs Arthur Gegg, Mrs Mary Gent, Mrs Marie Harman, Mr C W Harrison, Mr D M Hukin, Mrs F M Hunt, Mr E Jarrett, Wing Commander E R Johnston, Major J Jones, Mr Leonard T Jones, Mrs G M Key, Miss Ena Key, Mr Harry Leech, Mr Herbert Mann, Mrs E Marsh, Miss Ruby Miller, Mrs M Moore, Mr J D North, Professor A J Pippard, Mr R H E Pryce, Sir Alfred Pugsley, Mrs Alice Radcliffe, Mrs Florence Richmond, Mrs Doreen Rope, Mr C Rope, Mr Harold Rowe, Mr G F Simmons (Town Clerk of Bedford), Captain J A Sinclair, Sir Richard Southwell, Mrs Violet Steff, Mr W Stevens, Sir Henry Tizard, Mr Harry Tucker, Sir Frederick Tymms, Mrs Violet Turner (formerly Mrs Wilfred Moule), Mr L Turner, Lord Ventry, Major Oliver Villiers, Dr B N Wallis, Commander W H Watt and Mr W Whiting.

I would like to acknowledge the generous help given to me during my researches in France by M Joseph Bocquet, Secretaire of the Mairie at Allonne (Oise); M Leon Vasseur, the Adjoint of the Mairie and Mile Genevieve Bocquet.

My thanks are also due to the librarians of the Air Ministry, in particular to Mr J C Nerney, head of the Historical Branch of the Air Ministry; and to the libraries of the Royal Aeronautical Society and the Royal Aero Club Aviation Centre; and to Miss Mary Cosh and Mr Fred Dawson for helping me with the research involved. I am further indebted to Mrs Gent, Mrs Richmond and Mr Binks for kindly reading the manuscript of this book. Any errors still remaining are my own.

JL

Fifty-four people set out in R.101 on 4 October 1930.

There were six passengers:

Brigadier-General the Rt Hon. Lord Thomson, PC, CBE, DSO, Secretary of State for Air.

SirW Sefton Brancker, KCB, AFC, Director of Civil Aviation.

Major P Bishop, OBE, Chief Inspector AID.

Squadron Leader W Palstra, representing the Australian Government.

Squadron Leader W O'Neill, MC, Deputy Director of Civil Aviation, India, and representing the Indian Government.

Mr James Buck, valet to Lord Thomson.

Six officials were present from the Royal Airship Works:

Wing Commander R B Colmore, OBE, Director of Airship Development.

Major G H Scott, CBE, AFC, Assistant Director (Flying) Officer in Charge of Flight.

Lieutenant-Colonel V C Richmond, OBE, Assistant Director (Technical).

Squadron Leader F M Rope, Assistant to Assistant Dirertor (Technical).

Mr A Bushfield, AID.

*Mr H J Leech, Foreman Engineer.

There were forty-two officers and crew:

Flight-Lieutenant H Carmichael Irwin, AFC (Captain).

Squadron Leader E L Johnston, OBE, AFC (Navigator).

Lieutenant-Commander N G Atherstone, AFC (1st Officer).

Flying Officer M H Steff (2nd Officer).

Mr M A Giblett, MSc (Met. Officer).

G W Hunt (Chief Coxswain).

Flight-Sergeant W A Potter (Assistant Coxswain).

L F Oughton (Assistant Coxswain).

C H Mason (Assistant Coxswain).

E G Rudd (Rigger).

M G Rampton (Rigger).

H E Ford (Rigger).

C E Taylor (Rigger).

A W J Norcott (Rigger).

A J Richardson (Rigger).

PA Foster (Rigger).

W G Raddiffe (Rigger).

S Church (Rigger).

W R Gent (1st Engineer).

G W Short (Chargehand Engineer).

S E Scott (Chargehand Engineer).

T Key (Chargehand Engineer).

R Blake (Engineer).

C A Burton (Engineer).

C J Fergusson (Engineer).

A C Hasting (Engineer).

W H King (Engineer).

M F Littlekit (Engineer).

W Moule (Engineer).

A H Watkins (Engineer).

*AVBell (Engineer).

*J H Binks (Engineer).

*A J Cook (Engineer).

*V Savory (Engineer).

S T Keeley (Chief Wireless Operator).

G H Atkins (Wireless Operator).

F Elliot (Wireless Operator).

*A Disley (Wireless Operator).

A H Savidge (Chief Steward).

F Hodnett (Steward).

E A Graham (Steward).

J W Megginson (Galley Boy).

* Indicates survivors, of whom there were six.

CONTENTS

CHAPTER ONE
Day of Departure

All day, people had been arriving at the wide, bleak airfield above the town to see the airship leave, although she was not due away before evening. By late afternoon the field was churned into a sticky lake of mud, with the crowd, split now into small groups, all conversation exhausted, stamping their feet and turning their backs into the wind that swept in bitterly over the flat countryside. In the gathering dusk, lights glittered from Bedford and the weaving beams of car headlights turned as they approached in line, glittering more brightly as the sky grew darker. It was very cold.

The roads to the field had been blocked for hours with cars and motorcycles; earlier there had been special charabancs and coaches of sightseers so that, by six o'clock, more than three thousand people were already waiting huddled together in the bleak October rawness, and as many more were watching from parked cars round the airfield. A few newsboys, hoarse and wretched, called the late editions, and optimistic hawkers tried to sell picture postcards of the airship's lounge showing the ferns and plants in pots; and the promenade deck, which as in a sea-going vessel, had deckchairs for the passengers.

Above them all, shining silver and ethereal in the hard glare of many searchlights, hung the gigantic torpedo shape that was the reason for their journey, the world's largest airship, as long and as costly as an ocean liner, His Majesty's Airship R (for Rigid) 101, about to leave on her maiden voyage, to Egypt and on to India. A little apart from the main crowd stood the wives and relatives of passengers and crew who were going to fly in her on this first journey. Everyone shared the feeling of immense expectation and privilege; she had taken six years to build and most people in the neighbourhood had at least one friend or relative who had worked on her.

Now the moment of departure was near, and with it came a vast excitement; the future looked bright for Bedford and Cardington, the town on the hill and site of the Royal Airship Works where R. 101 had been assembled. Should this voyage be successful, it would be but the first of a regular British airship service, initially between Britain and India, and then to be extended so that it would girdle the Empire, with regular flights between Britain, Australia and Canada.

Since Cardington possessed the biggest airship mooring mast in the country, and incomparably the best facilities for maintenance, then, as an editorial writer of the *Bedfordshire Standard* had noted exuberantly when this airship plan had first been discussed some years previously: 'It is no extravagant stretch of imagination to assume that, with Cardington as the world's largest airport, this may mean the development of Bedford into one of the leading and most important cities of England.'

What this would mean in terms of work at a time of national depression in 1930 was enough to cheer the crowds out on the airfield and make them forget the bitter damp winds on this October Saturday. As one of them said afterwards: 'It seemed a wonderful thought, but somehow almost too good to be true.' Nevertheless, it gave comfort to many, for so severe was the depression around Bedford that often, when the great airship was 'walked' out of her shed, hundreds of unemployed men were given the job of holding on to the ropes that trailed from her side to prevent her becoming airborne and blowing away.

As each new car arrived bearing passengers or officials or just more sightseers, there was a fresh murmur of interest. People stood on tiptoe for a closer view of a door opening and the fixed smile of a man caught by photographers' flash bulbs. The whole scene seemed unreal and theatrical. To those already in the airship a hundred and eighty feet above them, the upturned faces of the crowd around the base of the mooring mast appeared like disembodied white discs stretching from darkness into darkness. They were anxious to be away.

The mooring mast at which the airship rode was a complicated tower of criss-cross girders, built like the Eiffel Tower in Paris. In the cluster of buildings on the ground, out of which the tower sprouted like a trellised steeple, a donkey engine blew fronds of steam into the damp darkness; it turned the winch that wound the airship into the cone at the top of the tower. There was little other noise, only an occasional cough in the crowd, the petulant honking of some official car, and the distant ring and echo of voices in the hollow emptiness of the airship coming down faintly.

Ground crew ran importantly up and down the two hundred steps in the spiral staircase, their boots clanging on the bare metal stairs. Other more distinguished visitors ascended in style in the lift. Lights blazed from the windows at the top of the tower where the lift opened into a circular room that, in turn, led out into a gallery. Close up against this gallery nestled the blunt round snout of the airship like the tip of some gigantic egg in its egg cup. A short covered gangway joined the two: the sides were carefully shielded with canvas so that no one unaccustomed to such heights should feel dizzy or nervous. This gangway was continued for about a hundred yards into the heart of the vessel until it opened out into a reception hall and other corridors to individual cabins. On either side of the gangway was a steadying rail, as on ocean liners, for R. 101 was an airship, and no effort had been spared to make the passengers' quarters as similar as possible to a liner's staterooms.

Major G H Scott, the Assistant-Director of Airship Development, who had been in charge of the training of the crew, stood a little apart from the rest, his curved pipe clamped between his teeth, wearing a new blue serge uniform for the first time. His cap bore the gold initials 'R.101', but apart from this he looked more like a naval officer than an airman. This was also no accident, for although they were technically part of the Royal Air Force, airship officers wore naval uniform with the cap badge of their craft. The crew were mainly civilians, but so that there should be uniformity on this voyage, they were dressed as Naval Petty Officers.

The airship service, of course, had long and close associations with the Navy. In the early days, during the First World War, volunteers were sought from the Navy to man the RNAS 'gasbags' or blimps' that patrolled the sea lanes on the watch for German submarines. Many airship officers had originally held commissions in the Navy, and the link persisted in a dozen ways. The vessels were *airships* steered by a coxwain with a ship's-type wheel; crew and passengers slept in bunks in cabins, many of which even had imitation portholes with electric light behind them. There was a promenade deck with a rail to lean on; left and right were referred to as port and starboard.

But in spite of his Navy-type uniform, Scott retained the Army rank he had held as commander of the British airship R.34, when she flew the Atlantic to America and back in 1919, the first airship to make the double journey. As Assistant-Director of Airship Development he was senior to Flight-Lieutenant Carmichael Irwin, who nevertheless commanded R.101: Scott decided such points as when she would sail, the course she would take, and her speed and altitude. Irwin, on the other hand, was in charge of the crew and carried out Scott's orders. Again, there was a Naval precedent for such an arrangement: Scott was in the position of an Admiral in his flagship; Irwin was the flagship captain and responsible for the discipline. Owing to the mixture of servicemen and civilians in each airship this was sometimes difficult. William Gent, for instance, his Chief Engineer, was an airship pioneer, one of the best-liked men in the crew, whose experience included working with Sir Hiram Maxim on aero engines in the early years of the century. Such was his popularity that all the crew called him 'Bill'. Irwin felt that such familiarity was not conducive to good order and discipline and circulated a note to this effect. Thereafter, the crew called him 'Chief' when Irwin was in hearing, and Bill when he wasn't.

Someone asked Scott what time he meant to start. (They knew the departure time well enough, but anything was better than to stand in silence in the cold, waiting for the minutes to pass.) Scott looked at his watch in his casual, unhurried way.

'We'll get away sharp to time, all right,' he replied. 'I want to prove that an airship can leave according to schedule.'

'Will you be able to take your pipe?'

Scott grinned, looking at it.

'I don't mind, one way or the other. I've spent so much of my time in airships already that I've grown quite accustomed to doing without tobacco when I'm in the air.'

This was quite true, and sometimes, even on land, he acted in a violent way towards anyone who lit a pipe or cigarette too near an airship. The danger of an explosion from the hydrogen that filled the gasbags within the airship was always so great that casual smoking could never be countenanced. Only a short time previously, Dr Hugo Eckener who, on Count Zeppelin's death, had become president of the Zeppelin Corporation in Germany, arrived at Cardington in his airship, the *Graf Zeppelin,* and one among the little knot of senior officers and officials waiting to welcome him took out a box of matches as if to light a cigarette. Scott saw the action and rushed at him, delivering a vigorous kick in the seat of his trousers that knocked him over. The unfortunate man struggled to his feet and apologized, realizing the enormity of his action.

Although, in R.34, Scott had indeed been forced to do without his pipe, R. 101 was unique in having a smoking-room. There, surrounded by five and a half million cubic feet of hydrogen that a spark could ignite, and only separated from it by the thin gasbags and a metal bulkhead, officers and passengers could sit back in safety in wicker armchairs and enjoy their pipes, or cigarettes and cigars. Nevertheless, everyone going on board was searched for matches, which were strictly forbidden. In the smoking-room there were cigarette lighters and ashtrays, but they were all chained to the tables, so that no one could carry them off absent-mindedly to his cabin for a last cigarette in bed.

On this particular night, the smoking-room was to have some distinguished visitors, for among those embarking on this great journey East were Lord Thomson, the Air Minister in Ramsay Macdonald's Labour Government, and Sir Sefton Brancker, the Director of Civil Aviation. The two men had much in common, for both were of military families, and had reached high rank in the Army - Thomson in the Engineers, and Brancker in the Gunners - until they fell in love with the air.

Sir Sefton Brancker, the more colourful of the two - and the more likeable - had arrived at Cardington much earlier in the afternoon, and had already spent some time talking with the wives of his fellow-voyagers. Many of the officers were carrying pith helmets, which had been issued only that morning as a precaution against the Egyptian sun. The incongruity of these Kiplingesque accoutrements on an English October afternoon drew some joking remarks from Sir Sefton. Always boyish, and with a great love of conjuring and practical jokes, Brancker used to produce toy balloons at parties and send them gyrating and squealing round the room. He was never seen without a monocle, which he wore from necessity, even on the polo field, and he used always to carry several spare ones, made specially for him without rims or cords, for his greatest parlour trick of all.

As a Subaltern in India, he had once vowed in the mess that if he were wrong over some subject, then he would eat his eyeglass. He was wrong, and he kept his word. Neither on that occasion, nor on any other, did his glassy diet have any ill effects. Only a few months before the R. 101 took flight, Brancker remarked to a friend: 'I got into the habit of eating glass and flew for bigger game, like vases or tumblers. I used to do it about once a fortnight, until I learned that powdered glass is a slow poison...'

For all his jokes, Brancker was one of the great pioneers of military aviation. As long ago as 1897, while still a Subaltern, he had gone up in a balloon at Lydd to observe artillery fire. He believed passionately in the future of aviation, and when he had a long journey to make he preferred to fly. To a man like this a trip by airship - the biggest, the safest, the latest in the world -should have been a commonplace. But Brancker held considerable private reservations about the usefulness of airships, which he believed could best serve as a stopgap in covering the long ocean routes while flying boats were being more fully developed. He also had much greater doubts about the wisdom of making this particular flight in this particular airship.

No one who saw him shake hands with Lord Thomson on his arrival knew what had passed between them only two days previously, at the Air Ministry. For the past month, as day-and-night work was going on at Cardington to get R. 101 ready for her flight East, Brancker, Scott and Wing Commander Colmore, the Director of Airship Development, had all become increasingly uneasy about the prospect. In their opinion, so Brancker told a friend, the airship was not really airworthy, and they wanted more trials before they left on such a long journey across the frozen Alps and the baking Egyptian desert.

Brancker was not a man to mince matters, so when Lord Thomson was in his office on the Thursday of that week, making final details about the flight, Brancker told him his own views on the matter. Thomson refused to believe him and said what he had already said so often, that he was pledged to go out and return in time for the Imperial Conference. Brancker protested that this did not seem to be a valid argument; if the airship was not fit to go, then Thomson should face facts and delay the departure.

'All right,' retorted Thomson, 'if you're *afraid* to go - don't! There are many others who will jump at the chance!'

This so annoyed Brancker that he at once walked out of the room; the two men had not met since. Now they met under the airship that had already darkened their association.

Brancker, bouncing, impetuous, slow to anger and quick to forget, had enjoyed a swift and successful career. Only a major in 1913, he was General by the end of the 1914-18 war and was knighted a year later.

On this afternoon, his pilot, Miss Winifred Spooner, flew him to Norwich, where he attended a luncheon of the Norfolk and Norwich Aero Club, for one of his enthusiasms concerned the need for local flying clubs and an airport outside every town. Miss Spooner was herself a pioneer pilot, and one of the few women to hold a commercial flying licence. Only the previous month she had been placed fourth in a gruelling air race round Italy.

After lunch, they flew down to Henlow and landed at half-past three, unable to come any closer to Cardington because the Air Ministry, ever conscious of the cost of their airship, had forbidden aircraft to approach within three miles of her while she was at anchor. At Henlow, therefore, Brancker transferred to a car, and Major O G G Villiers, an officer of his department and a personal friend for many years, drove him over to Cardington. Villiers had brought down some of Sir Sefton's belongings from his club earlier in the day; a few books he was taking to read on the journey and his topi.

As they drove through the flat countryside, Brancker suddenly turned to his colleague.

'I want you to do something specially for me,' he said. 'Amy Johnson is in a nursing home. Get her a big bunch of roses and give them to her with my love.'

Amy Johnson had just returned from a flight from London to Australia, and was suffering from delayed reaction from the flight; she had gone into hospital at Portsmouth.

'I've got some roses in my own garden,' Villiers replied. 'I'll pick some for her myself if you like.'

'Splendid. And don't forget to give her my love.'

The thought was typical of the man; anyone willing to further the cause of aviation was assured of his support.

Earlier that year, Lady Muriel Paget, noted throughout Europe for the welfare work she undertook in so many countries, had told Brancker that she was planning a trip to Russia, where she had organized the Anglo-Russian hospital in Petrograd during the war.

'You must fly,' he had said at once.

'I don't like long flights,' she explained. 'They make me ill.'

'Oh you'll be all right,' Sir Sefton assured her, minimizing her difficulty as he did all his own, and next day she received from his secretary not only particulars of all the air routes involved in the journey, but also a bottle of pills to reduce the risk of air sickness. And even while he was preparing for his own flight Brancker had dictated a message of congratulation to the Hon. Mrs Victor Bruce who was flying solo from England to Japan -the first person to do so.

'Hearty congratulations on a very fine flight,' he said. 'Your enterprise will be a fine example to other people in this country to do likewise. If we can persuade the sportsmen and sportswomen of Great Britain to travel to every country in the world in their own aircraft, we shall be establishing goodwill everywhere and proving the high standard of British aeroplanes and engines to everybody. Tomorrow I am off to India in R.101. The very best of luck to you...'

Sir Sefton went aboard early, meaning to come down and say goodbye to Major Villiers; but somehow he never did come down. He stayed looking down from the promenade deck through the celluloid windows let into the underbelly of the ship on the scene beneath him, as though entranced by it, and miles away.

Almost until the last moment he had expected the departure to be cancelled, for the weather was worsening and he knew the airship's history of working against time, and also that the few trials she had undergone had been made in perfect weather. Except for one occasion, when R.101 had stayed at her mast overnight in a thunderstorm, she had been kept cossetted in her gigantic shed whenever the wind was gusty. He knew all this and yet the knowledge did not appear to depress him.

Six years before, in the summer of 1924, when the British airship programme had not long been announced, he was lunching in Paris with a friend, and suddenly asked him why he did not have his horoscope cast.

'Have you had *yours* done?' the friend replied, surprised at the question.

'Yes. It says that I shall be quite alright for six years, anyway'

'And after that?' the friend persisted.

Sir Sefton removed his monocle and polished it.

'After that,' he said quietly, 'there is nothing to be seen.'

Lord Thomson, the Secretary of State for Air, and the only man - apart from the Prime Minister - who could have cancelled or postponed the flight, had also arrived early at Cardington. He went by train to Bedford from London, and then drove out to Cardington, in an official car.

'The only thing I fear is the journey to Cardington,' he would say when people asked about his views on flying. This was not quite accurate, for flying sometimes upset him; he would look pale when he stepped out of one of the bumpy, noisy aircraft of the day. A trip by airship was, of course, a different proposition, for her size and slowness made a journey a pleasure. There was hardly any noise, save for the creaking of the great girders, and little sensation of movement.

Reporters at once surrounded him as he climbed out of his car, for he generally had something to say that was worth quoting. With his urbane manner and his distinguished appearance, he cut an impressive figure as, parrying their questions, he smiled a politician's unworried smile. In the background, his valet James Buck busied himself with bags and grips.

'Will you make the entire journey?' one reporter asked Lord Thomson.

'Why not?' he retorted, answering one question with another, as though daring the man to give him a reason. 'I am under orders to be back in London by October 20, and I don't intend to have to change my plans.'

He did not find it necessary to add that there was indeed no imperative reason for his flying to India at all - save that he was determined to go. The orders he was under were his own.

He looked about the little group that had clustered round him.

'Unless something happens I shall go out and come back in the old bus,' he added. Then he made a motion towards the mooring mast, and at once the crowd parted obediently and let him through with his valet and their luggage.

At the entrance to the lift gates he met Colonel Vincent Richmond, the Chief Designer of the airship. The two men posed for pictures, Thomson willingly, looking up at the airship towering above; Richmond, more quizzically, with a sheaf of papers under his arm, anxious to be away from the limelight that so attracted his companion.

Richmond had motored out earlier that afternoon from his house at Odell, a few miles beyond Bedford. Usually his wife drove him, but on this occasion she had decided against driving his big Rover across the airfield and through the thick throng of people she knew would be there to see them off and had asked a friend to drive instead. Richmond's mother, approaching seventy years of age and a semi-invalid, but determined to see her son's airship leave, was also with them. Mrs Richmond and her friend helped her across the wet, trodden grass so that she could stand underneath the enormous belly of the airship her son had designed and look up at him when he went aboard. Both she and Florence Richmond were enormously proud of R.101. They, more than anyone, knew how much the airship meant to Vincent Richmond. They had lived with her from the first tentative rough designs. As he was about to step into the lift, he suddenly turned to his wife. 'Goodbye,' he said. 'Goodbye. And - keep the flag flying.'

Of the two men, Lord Thomson appeared more at ease; although only the day before, sitting at his desk in the Air Ministry, he had taken a sheet of notepaper from the drawer and made his will: 'In the event of my death during the flight of R.101 to and from India, or as a result thereof,' he wrote, 'I bequeath everything of which I die possessed - cash, shares, chattels and papers - to my brother Colonel Roger Gordon Thomson, CMG, DSO, of Springhill, Widdington near Newport, Essex.'

Lord Thomson was not a rich man; his assets then amounted to £1,737 - barely £1,000 more than his valet left in his will. He had, however, investigated the cost of insuring himself for the journey; the insurance companies regarded the risk of airship travel so lightly that they only asked a premium of 1 per cent. The Air Minister paid £5 and was insured for the sum of £500.

But there was no suggestion of any lack of confidence as he gave a smile here, a half salute to a friend in the crowd there, demonstrating at once his charm and his strength, for he was at home in this atmosphere, with crowds watching him and people to ask deferential questions.

He was delighted at the chance to make this pioneering flight to India by airship, for his life had been marked by spectacular chances which he had seized and turned to good advantage; and this journey, with its quality of high drama, seemed one of the most promising. He was already being mentioned as the next Viceroy of India, and what better than to arrive there by air, to show that the mother country, pre-eminent at sea, was also first in the conquest of the air?

An Imperial Conference had been called in London for later that October, and he wanted to step from the returning airship and drive straight to the meeting. This would be a far more telling way of promoting airships for the 'all-red' route to link the Empire countries than to rely on talk and plans. It smacked of action and decision, two qualities close to his heart. The Australian and New Zealand Premiers would have taken six or seven weeks at sea to reach London for the conference; he would be able to go to India and return to address the conference in less than half this time. That was the measure of the airship's speed, and her value in shortening Empire communications.

Lord Thomson had a personal reason for being interested in revisiting India, for he had been born there, the third son of a Major-General of the Royal Engineers, and but for his own genius in taking advantage of any chance he saw, young Christopher Birdwood Thomson - the famous Field Marshal was a relation - might have followed the conventional career of many of his contemporaries. He had, however, the priceless gift of always being able to recognize opportunity, no matter how heavily disguised it might come.

As a young lieutenant in the South African war, he had recognized it for the first time. Outside Kimberley, military operations were being delayed by a jam on the railway line, and General Kitchener, irascible and impatient as ever, wanted to know why. Thomson was apparently the only officer there with an engineering background, and so Kitchener ordered him to clear the line at once. A lesser lieutenant might have blundered and so blighted his chances for ever; not so Lieutenant Thomson, who realized there was only one way to carry out Kitchener's command - by doing what was wanted, however absurd that might seem, or however productive of later chaos. He ordered gangs of men to push the trucks on to their sides off the railway line, and so let Kitchener go through. As one astonished eyewitness remarked later, 'The trains and trucks were hurled forcibly off.'

Kitchener was so delighted at the speed, success and apparent simplicity of this operation - for possibly he had no idea how this unknown lieutenant could carry out his orders - that he spoke to Thomson a second time and told him of his pleasure. More important, he promised him his brevet-majority when he became a captain. From that day Thomson began to profit from his experiences and his postings.

As an assistant instructor at the Engineering School at Chatham, he learned how to address a critical and possibly hostile audience and turn them to his point of view. Later, as a member of the War Office staff, he learned how necessary politicians could be to an ambitious soldier, and how important it was for such a man to appear to bow to their wishes. Then, while they thought that they were getting their way, he knew that he was getting his. He also discovered how very important a soldier's friends could be.

One of his friends at the War Office was Sir Henry Wilson, Director of Operations, and when the First War broke out Thomson became head of the British Mission in Bucharest after Roumania joined the Allies. At the end of the war Sir Henry Wilson remembered this keen young engineer officer for whom nothing was too much trouble, and asked for his services on the Supreme War Council at Versailles.

Here Thomson, without private means, but with a native shrewdness that was far more valuable, became almost immediately at home. He grew to like the cosmopolitan world of what Americans call 'international do-gooders', and thrived in the strange atmosphere of resolution and amendment, of committee and sub-committee, and the inconclusive mist of recommendations that clouded so many of their meetings. He saw at once where his future lay, and with what some friends thought was a hasty, unconsidered gesture - but which was in fact nothing of the kind - Thomson resigned his commission and joined the British Labour Party.

Although naturally he was at first distrusted in his new surroundings because of his background, by his charm and most of all by his ability, he overcame this initial coldness on the part of traditional working-class Socialists, and again began to prosper. Thomson was one of the earliest converts to the Socialist cause to have a conventionally conservative upbringing; the eagerness of other ambitious men to identify themselves with the aims of the British working man had still to come. He had, therefore, the choice of many assignments for which, a few years later, competition might have been too sharp. He was presentable, educated and sincere, and the combination of these basic virtues brought him the chance of Labour Party missions to Ireland, to the Ruhr, even to Moscow.

The Committee of the Red Cross in Geneva appointed him Special Commissioner to inquire into the state of refugees in Europe, and Ramsay MacDonald became his friend. When the first Labour Government was returned to office in January 1924, Christopher Birdwood Thomson became head of the Air Ministry.

This for many might have been the end of all ambition; for Thomson it was only the beginning. He appeared to have a natural interest in aeronautical matters, especially in lighter-than-air craft as opposed to the more orthodox heavier-than-air aeroplanes. When the time came for him to be raised to the peerage, he showed the extent of this interest by taking as his title Lord Thomson of Cardington - the home of the Royal Airship Works, outside Bedford, where all State airships were constructed.

In December 1928 the London *Evening Standard* asked Lord Thomson to name what he felt would be the most important development over the next quarter century.

'In my view,' he replied, 'the most startling developments in flying during the next twenty-five years will be in connection with lighter-than-air vessels. I am aware that this opinion is not endorsed by many leading authorities on aeronautics, but it is based on the assumption that, where demand is consistent, supply must follow.

'The demand comes chiefly from the British Empire and the continents of North and South America, whose people require air communications across wide open spaces. These requirements can be met only by aircraft with capacity for non-stop flight of several hundred hours.'

Neither Lord Thomson nor others in his Ministry visualized that aeroplanes would ever possess this capacity so that they could cross continents in a fraction of the time the fastest airship would take - and carrying far more passengers. Events proved his prophecy to be wrong, but at least he was enthusiastic about flying and, like Brancker, used aircraft whenever he could. The Air Estimates soon showed this enthusiasm by rising nearly £3,000,000 - roughly 20 per cent above the Estimates of the previous year - and as Air Minister, he could indulge his love of travel by taking planes to Egypt, Palestine, Iraq, Transjordania and other places where Britain maintained air bases in those more Imperial years.

These journeys brought back something of the pleasant carefree unpredictability of service life in India before the First War. Back in London he would tell after-dinner stories of landings in the desert near the small concrete pillboxes that marked the position of petrol tanks buried in the sand. The Arab states had not then realized the benefits that the accident of oil beneath their ground could bring: the people were poor, covering vast expanses of shifting desert sands by camel, pitching their black nomadic tents around the small oases, and were friendly towards visitors from the skies. Once, at Suleimani, fifteen thousand of them came out cheering to meet Lord

Thomson and presented him with a horse on which he rode in state into the town. 'The procession was so long,' he said afterwards, 'that in circling the place its head met its tail.'

But he appreciated small gestures as much as gestures on such a grand scale. The small, unexpected kindness always moved him, and as he reached the base of the mooring mast at Cardington that Saturday afternoon someone handed him an envelope. He paused, and those who had attached themselves to him waited while he ripped it open. The letter was one of good wishes from Commander Sir Dennistoun Burney, who was responsible for building the private enterprise rival airship, R.100.

Lord Thomson showed his pleasure at being remembered, and he scribbled a reply as the people pressed round him. When Commander Burney arrived at his office in London on Monday morning it was there waiting for him at his desk: 'Many grateful thanks for your kind letter - Thomson.' Then the lift doors clanged and the lift began to rise.

Most of the crew had been working in the airship all day, with only a short dash home to say goodbye to their wives and families. William Gent had managed to cycle home for an early tea with his wife and Lawrence, their twelve-year-old son. Mrs Gent had been busy for a great part of the previous evening sewing his medal ribbons on his newly issued khaki drill shirts.

Engineer John Henry ('Joe') Binks had walked earlier from his lodgings at Shortstown to the main gate of the airfield in a more leisurely manner, and had then caught the bus on to the mooring tower gates, a penny fare away. The conductor, a local man who knew the crew, joked: 'If you're off to Betsy's it'll be another ha'penny'

Betsy's was their nickname for the Bell Inn at Cotton End, near the airfield, kept by Miss Betsy Bunker. Sometimes, during that long hot summer, when they were coming in to the mast in R.101 at the end of a day in the air, Chargehand Engineer George Short would call out, as though their friends could hear him at the Bell: 'Hold on, Betsy, we're coming!'

'How do you feel, Joe?' asked the gate warden as Binks arrived. 'You're looking very spruce.'

Binks felt as smart as he looked; he nodded and smiled, and walked up the road to the mooring mast, saving his breath for the run up the stairs, which he liked to climb without a pause. In the crew's hut near the mast he changed into overalls and then ran up the spiral staircase to the top. There, in the covered-in gallery, William Gent greeted him.

'Good morning, Joe,' he said, and as Binks paused for breath he added: 'You took your time coming up.' Joe grinned and picked up a drum of oil (kept in the gallery for topping up the engines) and carried it on the long walk right through the ship, and then down out of the envelope, down the swaying 'jumping ladder' suspended in the air below the great hull, and so into the rear engine car, for which he shared responsibility with Engineer Arthur Bell. Then he carried the empty drum back; up into the air, on into the envelope and back along the ship to the gallery. He decided the engine could do with still another drum, so he carried down a second one and then stood for a moment in his engine nacelle - the crew called these egg-shaped engine cars 'power eggs' - and looked around him. Everything was in order. The huge diesel engine crouched, polished and cold: the starting engine was ready to swing. The tools were in their racks: nothing was out of place, and the whole car seemed as shiny as a jeweller's shop.

He climbed up into the ship again to see that his fur-lined sleeping bag was laid out in the crew's sleeping quarters. There, among the ten pounds of personal kit he was allowed to carry, he had a bouquet of rosebuds wrapped in tissue paper and moistened with moss. His next-door neighbour in Shortstown was a keen gardener with hundreds of rosebuds about to bloom.

'Joe,' he had said that morning, 'I wonder if you'd take a few of these in your case to give to the ladies when you arrive at Ismailia?' In the crew room, heavy with the smell of dope from the fabric covering, the buds still kept their faint fragrance.

All this time, other members of the crew were arriving and exchanging greetings. When a chance occurred they went down to the ground level and had their lunch in the crew's hut - a fry-up of sausages, bacon and onions. As each new arrival entered and sat down he would ask: 'What are things like aloft? I suppose you've done all the work?' Others, their tasks done, their farewells said, played cards, anxious to be off. The crew were still taking stores on board, and also what seemed to some a vast stream of baggage, compared with the small allowance for the men. Each man's kit was weighed by an official in the customs house at the foot of the mast.

This was not done in the case of Lord Thomson's luggage, although he appeared to have more than anyone. The lift inside the mooring mast could carry the weight of twelve people, and all afternoon the lift attendant, Herbert Mann, had been busy ferrying people, baggage and stores to the top. When he came to deal with the Air Minister's baggage he needed two separate journeys to carry it all, and thus estimated that the luggage was equivalent to the weight of twenty-four people. Some cases were so heavy that they needed two men to carry them; he also had three or four large cabin trunks.

Photographers and reporters were making persistent efforts to climb on the ship, although what they could see or do there was doubtful, since there had been organized Press visits to her some time previously. Two photographers were actually brought down after climbing up 170 steps of the tower; no unauthorized visitors were allowed beyond the gates at the foot of the mast, and anyone who entered the lift was asked whether he had any matches in his pockets.

Engineer A H Watkins, at thirty-seven one of the older men in the crew - and only there because he had taken the place of another engineer at the last moment - suddenly realized as he was going up in the lift that he had forgotten to leave his matches in the crew hut down below, so he handed over a box of Swan Vestas to Mann, who put them in his pocket. Afterwards, on the impulse, Mann counted them: the box contained thirty-seven matches - one for every year of Watkins' life.

At least one of the passengers was also making the flight by chance. He was Squadron Leader W H L O'Neill, MC, who was described in the passenger list as 'representing the Indian Government'. This was not wholly an accurate description, although he was flying out to India to take up a new appointment as Deputy Director of Civil Aviation there, and his presence in the airship came about in this way.

Some time previously his wife, Elsie, had returned to England for an operation by Sir Henry Simson, the famous surgeon and gynaecologist to the Duchess of York (now the Queen Mother). O'Neill returned to England on special leave to be with his wife, but found that the operation had to be unavoidably postponed, because the Duchess of York was expecting a baby, so that Sir Henry Simson could for the moment accept no other cases.

This news completely upset O'Neill's arrangements, and he had to cancel his passage on the boat that should have taken him back to India. This was annoying, for he had already rented a flat in Calcutta and engaged a staff and even bought a pony for his wife out there, and it might be many weeks after her operation before he could book another passage East. Then one evening, in his club, he met Sir Sefton Brancker and happened to mention the circumstances that were keeping him in London.

'I'll tell you what we'll do, Bill,' said Brancker at once. 'We've got R. 101 going out to Karachi in a few weeks - probably just after your wife has her operation. If it's any help to you, I'll get you a passage on that.'

O'Neill knew all about R.101 and the rosy plans for her future, for his last posting had been in Karachi, at Drigh Road -now the site of the big Karachi Civil Airport - and he had watched with interest the building of the mooring mast and the great airship hangar which was to be both longer and higher than the one at Cardington. The idea of travelling on her maiden voyage, and also of saving time that was so valuable to him, had thus a double appeal. There were some delays before this passage was officially confirmed, for no ordinary fare-paying passengers were being carried, but at last he heard that the Indian Government would agree to his travelling in the airship as their representative.

O'Neill and his wife were in London with friends one evening while he was waiting for the reply from India; they had seen *Bitter Sweet,* and were in evening clothes on their way to the Savoy when he suggested taking a taxi by way of his club, so that he could go in and see whether there were any messages for him. In a few minutes he came bounding down the steps waving the cable of confirmation in his hand, and shouting excitedly, 'I've got it, I've got it!'

'I suddenly felt terribly ill,' said his wife afterwards, 'almost as though I was going to faint. I loathed the whole idea of Bill travelling on this airship, but I knew how keen he was on making the journey. I am a soldier's daughter, and I was an airman's wife. I didn't dream of letting him know my own secret fears about it.'

Sir Henry Simson and two colleagues successfully delivered the Duchess of York of Princess Margaret Rose at Glamis Casde on 21

August, and it was agreed that Mrs O'Neill should enter the West London Hospital shortly afterwards for her operation. Just before she did so, she and her husband were staying with old friends near Cardington, the Rector of Duxford and his wife. On an impulse they drove over to Cardington one weekend to see the airship, and O'Neill arranged permission for them to go aboard her.

'I loathed every moment of it,' said Mrs O'Neill. 'The Captain, Flight-Lieutenant Irwin, was aboard, and we were introduced to him. He seemed to me to be unusually pale - as pale as death. He came round with us to show us the quarters, and he kept on saying, "They're rushing us. We're not ready, we're just not ready."

'I felt miserable again all that evening, but I think if anyone noticed it at all, they put it down to my approaching operation. I felt so gloomy on the way back that I could hardly speak.'

Mrs O'Neill was making a successful recovery from her operation by the Saturday her husband left, but she was not well enough to come and see him off, so his mother and brother did that for her. 'Sky' Hunt, the Chief Coxswain, had been in the R. 101 since just after half-past three, and he watched O'Neill and other passengers come aboard. He was a burly man, looking even larger now in his white roll-neck sweater and flying boots. The side pocket of his uniform jacket bulged; it contained a packet of ham sandwiches his wife had made for him that morning.

Usually he went roaring around the ship, with a word of encouragement here, an admonition there, just as he went roaring around Bedford on his motorcycle; but this afternoon he was quiet. His arm, where he had been inoculated for the journey, was still sore, for one thing; and, for another, some of his confidence in the airship had diminished since he had seen her performance after she had been cut in two and lengthened by a new bay amidships.

'She can't be the same,' he had said gloomily. 'It's like fitting a new stomach into someone.'

Hunt was immensely popular with the crew, and one of the most experienced in all the airship service; his flying experience in lighter-than-air machines went back nearly twenty years. Earlier that day, as he ate a hasty lunch, all the neighbours had crowded into his house in South Drive, Shortstown, to wish him luck and to ask him to bring back some souvenirs; one of them wanted a parrot.

His wife, with their two children, Gwendoline, just two and a half and his son of fourteen, came down in the wet afternoon with Mrs Ida Potter, whose husband Walter was the Assistant Coxswain. 'Sky' Hunt was anxious that his son should join the Navy, for he had joined in 1910 as an AB Gunner, but the boy preferred a career in the Air Force. They were still discussing the pros and cons of each service when they reached the gates at the bottom of the mast, where they had to say goodbye.

'Well, son,' said Mr Hunt, as he shook hands, 'if anything happens to me, look after your mother.'

He had begun to climb up the steps slowly and awkwardly in his flying boots; there seemed more steps than usual. His wife watched him, and he turned and called down to her: 'Look after baby,' meaning Gwendoline. She nodded and waved in reply.

Farther across the field, Violet Steff, the wife of the Second Officer, Maurice Henry Steff, had brought their fourteen-month old daughter Joan to see her father leave. Mrs Steff was there with her friend Janita Daisy Johnston, whose husband was the navigator. Ernest Johnston was one of the most experienced navigators in the Royal Air Force, and had navigated the aeroplane in which Sir Samuel and Lady Maud Hoare had flown to India four years previously. He and Steff were in the strange position of holding similar posts in both the big airships, R.100 and R.101, a position that arose from the general shortage of trained men of their skill and calibre, and a natural Ministerial desire to economize on crew, since at no time were the two airships in the air simultaneously.

For the Steffs, a family reason had already made the afternoon noteworthy; their daughter had said the word 'Dad' for the first time. When Maurice Steff had left for Canada in R. 100 that July he had shaved off his moustache, for all the crew were dean-shaven - another leftover from Navy days - and he had also made all sorts of business and personal arrangements in case anything went wrong. This time he made no such provisions at all, for the R.101 was the biggest, safest, most modern airship in the world; nothing could go wrong.

Most of the crew spent what litde spare time they had that day with their families; Rigger Wilfred Moule had spent Saturday morning making his will. It was not that he felt any premonition of disaster, but he was a careful, cautious man; he did not like loose ends. Under the impression that he was insured for £750, which his wife Violet would receive if he met with an accident - a belief that others in the crew shared, although quite without foundation - he arranged for his bank account, about £30, to be divided between his father, his mother and his sisters.

When he left in the afternoon he assured Violet that all would go well in the flight. 'I'll be back in a fortnight,' he said. 'So don't worry. I will be all right. Take care of yourself.'

And then he left, convinced that she had nothing to fear financially, whatever should happen to him. In fact, she was left with nothing.

When Walter Radcliffe, another of the riggers (whose job was to climb the metal framework inside the smooth envelope and make adjustments or watch for gas leaks in the seventeen gigantic gasbags that supported the airship in the sky) reached home that lunchtime to say goodbye, his little son Alan was out playing in the park. Radcliffe went off on his cycle in search of him, for he was determined not to leave until he had seen him. The two were devoted: Alan would stay with his father for hours while he dug his allotment, and a special saddle had been fixed up for him on the crossbar of his father's bicycle so that they could go out together for rides. It was on this saddle that he rode back home from the park on that Saturday afternoon.

In the excitement of the departure, Mrs Radcliffe, who could not come down to the airfield to see the airship go because she also had a daughter of fourteen weeks to look after and no one to leave her with, did not think to tell her husband of an odd incident that had occurred in the morning. While his father was in the airship Alan had suddenly burst into tears and run into the kitchen where his mother was cooking breakfast.

'What's the matter, my little chap?' she asked him.

'I haven't got a daddy,' he sobbed.

'But of course you have, darling,' she said. 'Your daddy will soon be back.' She thought so little of the incident that she forgot all about it within a few minutes. Afterwards, she remembered.

Half-past six. It was dark now, and much colder. People's breath fanned out in pale fronds as they talked. In the distance a church bell struck; the noise carried clearly in the still air.

Four red lights started to flash from the top of the masthead to warn any aircraft unaware of the Air Ministry ban on close flying to keep away. They were not needed, for the whole airfield was such a blaze of light from searchlights and car headlamps, that the glow could be seen for miles. One red light on top of the tower cast a reddish glow over the blunt, smooth nose of the airship, and green and red navigation lights began to glitter on the fins. The control car was already brilliant with inside lights, and a softer, yellow glow from the windows of the dining-room showed that preparations were already ahead with the evening meal for the passengers. ('Only a cold meal tonight,' an official told an inquirer.)

The gangway was closed, for all were aboard. Some reserve members of the crew who were not flying stood a little apart from the rest on the ground, looking up, envying those who were.

Two men who had been offered positions in the crew - one as a chef and the other as a rigger - were not on board because they had each asked for £1 a week more than they were offered. The chef, Charles Nesbitt, had flown to Canada as a chef in R. 100 and for this trip he was offered £3 a week. He asked for £4, but it had been refused, pending an inquiry, and so he was left behind. The cook who was travelling, Eric Graham, felt so pleased with the chance of making the flight that he had turned down £50 from an acquaintance to change places with him for this journey.

In the control car a small light flickered on and off impatiently. Everyone was waiting for the airship to move, but still she hung in the darkening sky. Lights were also on in the gondola, and the crowds recognized Brancker, Thomson and Richmond as they leaned over the rail of the promenade deck looking down at the pale sea of faces. Under the intense searchlights the silver hull glittered as though burnished; the trampled grass a hundred and eighty feet beneath seemed greener in their glare.

In the little engine cars hanging from their struts beneath the hull the engineers waited, ready to crank the small starting motors that would turn the big diesel engines. These cars were very cold until the engines began to run, and then the heat and noise were unbelievable. All the engineers were issued with earplugs against the bellow of the exhausts, but they rarely wore them, for they made speech impossible, and the tinkle of the engine telegraph difficult to hear.

The propellers were at the rear of the engine cars, and from their hubs a steel cable ran to a point in the hull about fifty feet further back to help take the strain of pushing the airship along. A small propeller was fixed to the front of each car, to be driven by the wind for charging the batteries.

The cars themselves were very cramped. The huge eight-cylinder diesel engines, based on engines originally developed for a Canadian railroad company, took up most of the available space; the rest was shared by the Engineer and a petrol starting engine, which itself could be irritatingly difficult to start, especially at higher altitudes. The engineers had two apertures in each engine car through which they could see that both propellers were turning freely. These slits also offered some ventilation.

A trapdoor in the roof of each 'power egg' led out by way of a steel ladder to the airship for the engineers to use as they relieved each other on duty. The smell of petrol, needed for the starting engines, was almost overpowering in the confined space. Wrapped up against the cold the engineers peered out of their small windows trying to see what was happening beneath, anxious now to be away and airborne. The sooner they were away, the sooner they would be back.

Watching them without envy from the ground was a young man who had flown as engineer in R.100 to Canada that summer. He had been asked to fly on this trip as well (for like Steff and Johnston, some of the crew were interchangeable), but he had refused. A short time later, and very thankful he had not gone, he was out on his motorcycle and collided with a lorry. He died at once.

The telegraph rang again. The engineers, two on duty in each car, as was the procedure while starting, turned on their petrol, and then began to swing the starting handles against compression. The starting engine in the starboard engine car was the first to go, running slowly, backfiring, sounding like a motorcycle in the sky. In went the Bendix gears that connected the spinning cranks to the diesel engine. Slowly the propeller turned, but still the big diesel engine would not catch. The auxiliary engine stopped again under the strain, and was restarted.

This time the propeller went round, still jerkily but with more strength, and the tower commander, Captain F G Cook, ordered Mann to take the lift to ground level and wait for extra cylinders of gas that might be needed to help start the engines. They were being brought from the gas station. While he was waiting for them, the wife of Tich' Mason, an Assistant Coxswain, pushed through the barrier and rushed over to the lift, sobbing; she begged Mann to take her last letter up to the tower to her husband. Mann hesitated. He had his clear instructions; to stand by, to wait for the gas bottles, but nevertheless he found it hard to resist this urgent appeal. He looked out across the dusk towards the gas station; no vehicle was yet in sight. By the time one could arrive he would be down again. He took the letter up, and handed it to someone standing at the airship entrance.

Underneath the airship, the crowd were beginning to stamp their feet, impatient now for something dramatic to happen. A few drifted away over the soggy ground; motorists, fearing a jam at the gates, were starting their cars.

Almost unexpectedly, the big airship motor began to run, lumpily at first, blowing out dark gouts of smoke from its exhaust. Bells tinkled in the other engine cars, and soon all were running smoothly, warming up, the thunder of the exhausts terrifyingly loud to those underneath.

Up aloft, Chargehand Engineer Short shouted down to Binks and Bell in the after-car: 'All right, Arthur? All right, Joe?'

They shouted back, one after the other: 'All right, Shorty.' Everyone was impatient to be off now.

Someone else shouted irritably: 'When the hell are we going? What's happening?' 'Let's pack up and go to Betsy's, Arthur,' suggested Binks jokingly. Anything to speed the moment of departure.

In the lower control car, which was slung beneath the airship like a single-decker tramcar, Flight-Lieutenant 'Bird' Irwin, the captain of the airship, stood at the controls awaiting the moment to cast off. This car was only about twenty feet long, for the main control room was actually inside the body of the airship, next to the wireless room - an unusual arrangement peculiar to the airship. Two control cars meant a good deal of running up and down ladders between them and did not make for efficiency or ease in handling. In R. 100, there was only one large control car, in which the navigator also worked, and the captain could know where he was in an instant, but in R. 101 he had to run up a ladder to find out. When they were flying at night he could, of course, fling out flares to see where they were. These flares were also used for taking compass bearings and to calculate drift.

The advantage claimed for having two control cars was that the one underneath the airship could be small and so offer less wind resistance. The designers of the *Graf Zeppelin* and R.100 did not subscribe to this theory. In those airships, too, the engines were all behind the control car and the passengers' quarters; in R.101, two engine cars were in front, with a consequent increase in noise which blew back as the airship flew along.

The upper control car contained the chart table and all the navigating instruments, including a sextant, which was rarely used. When it was wanted, an officer had to carry it along the ropewalks that ran within the vast dark hull and out of a small trapdoor in the upper part of the bows. He could then walk along the top of the vast envelope and 'shoot the sun'. This was safer than it sounds, for the airship could slow down while he was thus engaged, and, in fact, people often walked along the top of the airship, for exercise or for the view, while she was in flight. Nevil Shute, the novelist, who worked as a calculator on the construction of the airship R. 100, recalls that Commander Burney once dropped his watch when he was aloft on the top of that airship. It stayed there all night in a dip in the canvas until a rigger, out early the next morning, found it and returned it to him.

Flight-lieutenant Irwin stood in the centre of the lower control car, tall, pale, tense and tired. He shared with Squadron Leader Ralph Booth, who commanded R.100 (and who was even then down among the crowd, looking up at his rival, comparing her departure with his own that summer in R. 100 for Canada) the distinction of being the most senior airship captain in the country. As a commander of non-rigid airships at East Fortune, the Scottish airship station, Irwin had enjoyed the reputation of having the smartest ship. If an engine had to be changed in any airship there, some commanders allowed the work to be done in daylight. If it happened on Irwin's airship, the job was done at night so that no flying time should be lost.

He was a great athlete and on several occasions had run for Ireland and the Royal Air Force. He did this with the tremendous determination with which he did everything; but the result had tired him.

'Never let your boy go in for too much sport,' he used to tell Gent, his Chief Engineer. 'It will only strain his heart and tire him out'

Irwin had another reason for being tired on that Saturday night, apart from the continual worry of preparing his giant airship against time. He had been studying in his spare time for his Air Force promotion examination. As a lighter-than-air-pilot, he found the procedure of flying heavier-than-air aeroplanes something to be studied with care. Airship crews still used many terms of nautical origin; aircrews did not.

And above all this, Irwin was Irish and fey. He did not feel at all confident about the successful outcome of the journey. There were too many imponderables, too many hasty decisions, too many changes. Their total was one of doubt as he stood in his control car watching the minutes tick away, for to add to them were the late weather reports that all spoke of wind and rain to be expected. All wisdom, all experience urged that they should postpone their flight, for the airship had not done a trial at full speed, and indeed had only been flown on short journeys in ideal flying conditions, but Lord Thomson was determined that they would leave as announced, and would not change his mind.

Although the car was small it was cold; no heating came on until the generators were running. To Irwin's front the Steering Coxswain stood, holding the round wooden spokes of a ship's type wheel. His eyes were not on the scene beneath, which he could have clearly seen through the tall narrow windows with which he was surrounded, but on his compass and altimeter which were facing him. His would be the responsibility for holding the airship to her course. To him, these were the most important instruments on the airship.

To his right, by a side window, stood the Height Coxswain, responsible for the up and down motion of the airship. He had a similar wheel, set sideways along the wall of the car, and connected by wires and pulleys to drums that controlled the elevators. On the left-hand side of the car was a control panel with handles or toggles that released ballast from the tanks spaced round the ship so that, at a touch, the load at the bows could be lightened for take-off, or the tail of the airship trimmed if she began to feel tail-heavy while in flight. The control of the ballast and weight in a vessel of this gigantic size was so important that each of the thirty-eight main fuel tanks was fitted with circular cutters which worked on the principle of the cutter incorporated in the lid of a round tin of cigarettes, so that in an emergency the tank's 224 gallons could be emptied in three seconds.

From other toggles on the control panel wires ran to the emergency ballast bags in the bows of the airship, amidships, and in the stern. These bags were made in the shape of an enormous pair of trousers - and Zeppelin crews actually called them *lederhosen* (leather trousers). These 'trousers' were full of water, and when the wire was pulled one leg would drop and discharge its half ton of water, or whatever the amount might be. This crude system was remarkably effective in that it was swift and, so long as the wire did not break or foul some part of the structure, it was also foolproof. Manipulating the toggles was called 'playing the organ'.

When the airship was in flight, the ballast tanks, holding eight tons weight of water, were replenished during rain or in wet clouds by opening scoops on the airship's upper surface which collected moisture. They had to be replenished in some way for as the engines consumed the fuel oil the airship would naturally become lighter and so would tend to rise. During the First War airships had flown with no water ballast and with all their tanks full of fuel to give them greater range, but in peacetime this was frowned on, reasonably enough, as being both dangerous and expensive if any had to be released. A sudden discharge of a hundred gallons of brown fuel oil from a few hundred feet up could also be most unpleasant for anyone who happened to be underneath at the time, although a great deal of fuel thrown out like this did vaporize before it reached the ground and from greater heights there was total vaporization. The R. 101 was carrying 25 tons of fuel oil on that Saturday night.

As Irwin gave the order to increase engine speed, so that he could feel the airship pull against the cone into which her nose nestled at the masthead, a cheer from the crowd came up thinly to those aboard.

Up at the top of the mooring mast Mann, the lift operator, heard the telephone begin to ring. Captain Cook answered it.

'Stand by to slip,' came the order from the control cabin. Cook gave the order to Chargehand-Electrician Brewster, who waited to release the airship from her mooring. A moment of tense silence followed, Cook standing with the phone at his ear.

Then: 'Slip!' came the crisp command from the control car.

'Slip!' echoed Cook.

Brewster whipped out the pin securing the release lever and then jerked it down, releasing the airship's retaining safety wire, so that she was free of the cone, the tower and all contact with the earth.

'All engines full speed astern,' said Irwin into his voice-pipe.

Again the telegraphs rang in the engine cars; the Engineers pulled open their throttles, and the great diesels began to thunder. As R. 101 pulled out of the cone at the masthead, her bow should have soared up, but instead it dipped slightly. She was so heavily laden with extra fuel oil for the 3,000-mile journey to Egypt and with passengers and their luggage, that she had no resilience left. Also the concave surfaces of the top panels had been gathering moisture all day and this accumulated water added greatly to the gross weight. Even such a small dip was dangerous, for she was at most a hundred and eighty feet - the height of the mast - above a crowd of thousands, and her total length was seven hundred and seventy feet. A relatively small dip could bring her bows down among the spectators, for Irwin had no height at all for manoeuvring.

He had not a second to lose; he had to bring her nose up again, at once. The only way was to release ballast from her bows - which would leave him without much more to let go should her bows become heavy again in flight. No matter. If he did not release it immediately, there might not be a flight. Irwin gave the order.

The water sprayed out into the air in great gouts, and caught the light in a million tears, reflecting it like a cascade from some fairy-tale fountain. The wind from the spinning propellers vaporized it, blowing this strange cold rain down on the upturned faces of the watchers.

'She's moving!' someone shouted. So she was; sluggishly and heavily, like a ship that has taken water and is weary before the voyage begins. Others took up the cry, but most of the people were so cold and damp and wretched that they did no more than wave. A boy of eight in the crowd began to scream hysterically, shrieking wildly as the noise of the engines increased, and their roaring acted like a trumpet call: people began to cheer more loudly, stamping their feet and clapping their hands with excitement as slowly, heavily, almost casually, the great airship began to back away from the mast.

'Why, Mrs Gent, you're looking very glum,' said a neighbour whose husband was not flying, suddenly seeing who was standing next to her. 'Can't you raise a smile?'

'No,' said Mary Gent sadly, 'I can't.'

As the engines accelerated, the long airship trembled slightly as though throwing off a fever, and then she went on more steadily in the glare of the lights.

At this sign of positive departure the crowd gave another cheer that was heard above the bellow of her engines. Drivers of the cars that stretched in an unbroken line down the road to Bedford flashed headlights on and off in farewell. Up aloft the crew could hear the farewell shout of 'Sky' Hunt: 'We're away, lads! The ship's away!'

From his car Joe Binks could see the mooring tower: not as he wanted to see it, clearly, but through a haze of rain. And the airship, instead of lifting dear away from the tower, was now falling back a little to port with her tail sloping downwards.

The telegraph rang with an order from the control car: 'Halfspeed.'

At last R. 101'lifted her nose above the masthead, and when she was clear, began to move forward into the darkness, the roar from the engines increasing, the searchlights still holding her as she crept away. Another cheer went up, and many people praised the caution of captain and crew. They thought this slowness was an attempt to keep the vessel steady so that the passengers should not be disturbed by the motion in the rising wind. Few of those who saw her circle the airfield had any idea that she was going so slowly because she could not go any faster.

'I feel uneasy about her,' Mrs Potter admitted to Mrs Hunt, as they watched her go. Almost as she spoke, 'Sky' Hunt leaned over the side of the control car, flashing his torch towards them. It was a prearranged signal. His little daughter Gwendoline called up against the thunder of the engines: 'Goodbye, Daddy!'

The crowd was now also moving away from the mooring mast, stumbling in the darkness, for their eyes were fixed on the departing airship and not on the potholes and ruts in the field. Many with friends and relations aboard her cheered and waved, as though the crew could see them in the darkness. Some people even began to sing, and Mrs Gent, who was walking across the field with her son, Laurence, and Louise, the wife of his chargehand, Sidney Scott, suddenly remembered that after a holiday in Jersey that summer, they had brought back a duty-free bottle of cherry brandy. As they all walked towards the road, Mary Gent thought it would be a fitting farewell if she asked Louise home so that they could drink a toast to the departing airship and to the safe return of all those aboard her. As she was about to suggest this, however, Laurence said something and the idea went out of her head. Later, she was glad.

Red and green navigation lights twinkled as the airship turned, and then she slid through the dark sky beyond the hold of the searchlights. For a long time the patient watchers could see tiny stabs of light from some of the windows; the crew were signalling with torches to their families and friends. Then the throttles opened again and the diesel engines began to roar. As she moved, the shape of her hull was lost so that soon only the glow of her lights in the passenger lounges could be seen like the windows of a railway carriage in the sky. She circled Bedford, dipping her nose in a salute of farewell, her lights for a moment illuminating the High Street, the Embankment and the shining river beyond.

Then she lifted her nose as a ship rises to meet an oncoming wave, and slid out into the darkness towards the south-east of the town. Only the faint dying roar of her engines remained, with the heavy smell of oil in the damp air. As time went on, the rain, so long awaited, began to fall; lightly at first, and then more heavily. The wind rose violently. It was going to be a rough night.

1. A contraction of their official title: 'B' type, limps - as opposed to rigid airships which had a rigid metal frame.

CHAPTER TWO
Point of Inception

Once the airship was clear of Cardington and heading southeast at a rather laborious 25 miles an hour and a height of 1,500 feet, all aboard experienced a feeling of relief. At last they were actually airborne, on their way and on their own, finally free of all the bickerings, the worries, the constant nagging of critics and the race against time which had marred that summer. True, their speed was only about a third of what had been hoped from the R.101, but the night was bad and they faced a long and difficult journey; they were wise to conserve their engines.

The theoretically perfect flying height for an airship was two and a half times her own length, but the Captain was powerless to increase his altitude greatly for a reason peculiar to airships as vessels that depended on being lighter than the air that surrounded them. If he decided to climb, then the gas inside the gasbags would expand as the pressure of the air outside grew less. This meant that the gas valves would automatically open -for if they did not the bags would burst. But with each cubic foot of gas that escaped, the airship would lose the same amount of 'lift', and so by a fearful paradox, in trying to gain extra height the Captain would instead lose it. As he had already spilled about three tons of gas in rising from the airship's pressure height of 1,000 feet - the height at which the gas expanded to fill the bags without any overflow - to the cruising height of 1,500 feet, he was naturally loath to lose any more, for he had no means of replenishing gas lost until he reached Ismailia which, on that Saturday night, seemed an uncomfortably long distance away.

Nor were the crew cheered by a radio message from the Meteorological Department at Cardington which warned them to expect winds of between 40 and 50 miles an hour - a velocity that no British airship had ever previously encountered over land, and actually twice as fast as the winds they had expected to meet. However, they could not turn back; they had to go on, although they began to lose height to a degree that alarmed some observers on the ground.

Mrs Shane Leslie, wife of the well-known author, was dining at her home near Hitchin that evening when she suddenly heard her servants scream. 'Everything was lit up by a ghastly red and green light,' she later told the *Daily Express.* 'We rushed out - and there was the R.101, aiming straight for the house. She was so low it didn't seem as if she could miss it. I said, "Well, this is the end of my cottage," and rushed over the nearest fence, while the servants scattered in the other direction. She cleared the trees of our drive and the house by the smallest margin. I never thought she would make it. We could see the people dining, and the electric bulbs in the ceiling. She seemed to be going very slowly, and her engines seemed weak and unbusinesslike. I suppose we are the highest point (600 feet) she had to pass before she crashed. As the green and red tail lights moved away up the drive, horror descended on us all, in spite of the sudden relief of escaping what we thought was certain doom.'

For the time being, however, although the weather was far from ideal for flying, and although both their height and speed as they approached London were lower than some might have wished, there was little anxiety on board. They were pathfinders, the blazers of a new Imperial air route that would bring Egypt within a two-day and Bombay within a five-day journey, and eventually make all the world a smaller, friendlier place. Although in distance they might only be a few miles from their starting point, their thoughts were already ahead, dwelling on the first stop at Ismailia.

Each, in his own way, on his own level, from Air Minister to Chief Steward, had a reason for wishing they were already there. For Lord Thomson, waiting to sit down to dinner in the wide dining-room, with the glasses all stamped with Royal Air Force wings, and crockery stacked on the dresser - for the airship usually travelled so gently and so steadily that the cutlery did not even rattle - the reason was partly political. The High Commissioner for Egypt, with various senior British and Egyptian officers, was coming to dine aboard His Majesty's airship - just as they had so often dined in the past aboard one of His Majesty's warships. This would be the first time that such a dinner party had ever been held in the air, for the airship would be riding at anchor from the new mooring mast at Ismailia, a hundred and eighty feet above the ground. It would indeed be an historic and Imperial occasion worthy of the most detailed preparation, and so that none of the essential pomp and circumstance should be lacking, heavy carpets and loads of special silver had been taken aboard some time before they left Cardington.

Because of this dinner, and also, no doubt, because of the distinguished passengers who were travelling, the 600-foot long corridor that ran from the door in the bows of the vessel to the cabins within, had been covered with a pale blue Axminster carpet. Similarly, the floor of the lounge, which was as large as a tennis court, had been fitted with an enormous carpet of the same colour. This added weight did not please those who knew the slender margin of safety the airship possessed at the best of times, in ideal weather and flying conditions. Lieutenant-Commander Atherstone, the First Officer, gave this news to his wife Eve as she saw him off at the base of the mooring mast, and then remarked rather wryly: 'A layer of dust an eighth of an inch thick on top of the airship is said to weigh a ton, so you can imagine what this means to our load.' In an attempt to scrap other disposable weight, the crew had been ordered to leave their parachutes behind at Cardington.

Crates of champagne and barrels of beer embossed with the crossed flags of Britain and India had also been carried aboard, and with desperate ingenuity no less than twenty excellent varieties of cheese had been blended to produce something original for the dinner party. The steward responsible for this singular concoction claimed that its preparation had compelled him to eat nearly two pounds of cheese a day as he sampled the various kinds submitted by firms eager for publicity. 'After such a feat of endurance,' he said later, 'you can imagine that I do not much fancy *my* dinner.'

That was by the way; the main thing was that the guests and passengers should fancy theirs. Indeed, this state dinner, which now occupied the thoughts of the stewards, had caused a radical change to be made in the plans for fuelling the airship. When the flight to the East was first proposed, the original plan had been to take on more fuel oil at Ismailia, but clearly this could not be done while such an important dinner was in progress, for refuelling was a messy, noisy business, and the richer the meal the more deadly would be the effect of the heavy sickening smell of oil. Nor would there be much time to refuel after dinner, because the airship was scheduled to leave for India at about four o'clock in the following morning, so that she could miss the inversion belt over the desert. In hot climates the gas expanded and gave greater lift, while at night or in cloud or cold air the gas contracted and the airship had to discharge her ballast to hold height at all. It was believed that there might be a danger of her foundering in these conditions, and in the heat the gas in the great gasbags would also expand and make her heavier to handle in the evening. This accounted for the urgency in giving her more 'lift' by pumping more gas into the bags, stripping away inessential fittings and finally lengthening her so that another gasbag could be added. Even with these modifications, that had occupied most of the summer, an early morning departure from Ismailia was essential, and so it was decided to carry as much fuel as they could so that as little time as possible would be spent taking on more at Ismailia. Thus R. 101 was loaded with 25 tons of diesel oil, although under favourable conditions she should have been able to reach her destination on about 16 tons. Ten tons of this fuel oil was contained in the tanks fitted with cutters or other quick-release valves.

In the little galley, set behind the passengers' quarters and reached by a hazardous journey along a nine-inch-wide catwalk, 'Ernie' Savidge, the Chief Steward, was preparing the evening meal. The worries of the state dinner in the sky could be set aside for the time; he had plenty of immediate concerns, not least the knowledge that rainwater was leaking into the galley in some unexplained but most uncomfortable way, and that if he inadvertently switched on all his electrical equipment at once he was in grave danger of fusing the whole airship.

Savidge had worked for years in ocean liners - in Cunard and Union Castle ships, and also in ships of the old White Star Line, but although the size of these great ships might be comparable to R. 101, the conditions under which he worked were not. In the airship, as in R. 100, in which he had flown previously, he had one electric oven and a stove with a hot plate and a steamer for vegetables. On the other side of the tiled galley was a sink with a cold-water tap, and a geyser; a small table; and shelves packed with glasses and china. A lift stood ready to take up the cooked meals to the dining-room above.

This might seem sparse equipment with which to prepare a meal for a hundred people - the theoretical number of passengers the airship could carry - but the wonder was not that he had so little equipment, but that he had so much, for alloys were not so far advanced then as they are now, and a kitchen range was a heavy article to install in a lighter-than-air machine. Megginson, the galley boy, was helping him to prepare the meal, as he had helped him on the successful flight across the Atlantic in R. 100 that summer. At eighteen, he was the youngest member of the crew and intensely keen on his job and proud of his position. When his mother had questioned the wisdom of making such a voyage, he had retorted: 'But look at the adventure, mother, I'll be all right, and I'm the lucky one.' So it seemed at the time, for five hundred young men had applied for the job.

That night, dinner was cold; the R.101 galley had, in fact, rarely seen a meal cooked for a full complement of passengers and crew, and it was very difficult to prepare such a meal. When one had been attempted on such a scale - in November of the previous year, for a visit of a hundred members from both Houses of Parliament to inspect the airship - subterfuge had been resorted to. Much play was made of the fact that these guests would have a four-course meal in the air - which indeed they enjoyed - but no one said where the meal was actually cooked. Fortunately for the sponsors of the lunch, bad weather at the last moment made a flight impossible, and so the visitors, fifty at a time, sat down in the dining-room while the airship rode at her mooring mast, which made it much easier to provide their lunch. Royal Air Force cooks simply prepared the food on the ground, and then 'boilers' containing the hot lunch of oxtail soup, roast chicken with bacon, bread sauce, potatoes, green peas and gravy, with jam tart and rice pudding, were carried up to the top of the tower and humped down the catwalk to the galley. There they were unloaded, dished up, and put into the service lift that connected the galley to the dining-room. The three stewards on the airship's strength could not possibly cope with so much to carry and so many to serve, and outside volunteers were called in. One of them, Mr James Collingwood, who was then a journeyman baker, still remembers his excitement at being asked to help. 'No one ever suspected what we had in those boilers,' he says.

Presumably a similar arrangement for cooking the Egyptian dinner was planned with Royal Air Force cooks from Ismailia. The Egyptian guests would doubtless have been deeply impressed by the airship, for size possesses a fascination that is almost hypnotic.

The entrance hall, with the main staircase leading to the cabins and the lounge, was very like that of a great ship. The great white-and-gold lounge in which the passengers could take their ease was originally designed to accommodate a hundred people and measured 60 foot by 33 foot, the largest compartment ever to be constructed in any airship. Some of the pillars that gave added dignity to the surroundings were covered in Royal blue velvet, and wicker seats with pneumatic cushions lined the walls. Small moveable tables, like card tables, with wicker easy chairs were in the centre of the room for writing or card games, and the airship was usually so smooth in flight that these loose chairs and tables showed no tendency to slide across the floor. At the far end of the lounge, which had huge potted palms in the corners, three steps led up to a deck where passengers could sit in deckchairs and look down through long, wide celluloid windows at the country over which they were flying. At night, curtains could be drawn across the open doorway on top of the steps, and also across the windows that separated the lounge from the promenade deck. A rail was provided on the promenade deck for passengers to lean on as they admired the view, and to stop anyone falling overboard if the airship lurched or rolled unexpectedly. The pillars that supported the ceiling in the lounge were of light metal, cunningly covered with balsa wood and those not draped in velvet were so finished that a casual glance would take them for solid carved wood. But much of the care that had gone into their construction - which combined a minimum of weight with the appearance of solidity was nullified by the fact that metal tubs had been built around their base and filled with earth for potted plants.

Passengers slept two to a cabin in ship's-type bunks, one up and one down. These bunks had sides of thin, strong netting to prevent a restless sleeper from pitching out on to the rug that lay on the polished floor, and at the end of each cabin facing the door, was the imitation porthole. Under the bottom bunk, towards the foot, hot air was blown through a metal grating from a complicated system of ventilation pipes. This was essential, since the airship, being so large and covered only with the thinnest skin of fabric, with currents of air continuously and purposely blown in from the bows as she travelled along, to keep the air pressure inside the same as that outside, always felt bitterly cold, even in warm weather.

Under the imitation porthole in each cabin hung a notice with instructions on the procedure for ringing for a steward. It did not mention the procedure during an emergency; the airship was held to be so safe that no emergency could possibly occur. Beneath this again was a small, collapsible stool with a canvas top strong enough to take a passenger's suitcase. There were no doors, only thick curtains that could be drawn across, and each cabin was numbered.

This journey was by far the greatest ever to be made by a British airship, even more ambitious than R.100's crossing to Canada four months before. Hitherto, although balloon and airship flights had been made regularly since 1910, particularly (and most successfully) by the Germans, and although airship construction was advanced in America, which had a monopoly of the non-inflammable gas, helium, British airships had not been notably successful. The peak of their achievement had been reached in the war when they had been used for convoy work, to spot submarines (for their engines could be stopped and restarted in mid-air, and thus they could hover in silence above the sea lanes. The Germans had used airships for bombing attacks on British cities. A German Zeppelin had already flown around the world, but since the East was still synonymous with riches - and possibly the greatest investment of British capital was then in India - that country was the destination of this first journey of the R.101, just as the merchant adventurers of the Elizabethan age had sailed East in their voyages of enterprise.

The R. 101 was intended to change the story of misfortune that had characterized so many earlier attempts to build successful airships in Britain, and with this in view her size was comforting. She was so large that even before her construction could be started the existing airship shed at Cardington had had to be extended in length from 700 feet to 800 feet, and raised in height from 110 feet to 157 feet, an increase that made it the largest building in the British Empire. The airship was equally enormous. She contained two miles of longitudinal steel girders, six miles of booms, or smaller girders, and eight miles of side and base struts, making 18,000 struts in all. The bracing cables that pulled in her huge sides represented a total length of 11 miles; and she carried 12 miles of webs and 27 miles of tubing of various kinds. Four hundred and fifty thousand rivets held together this flying Leviathan.

The seventeen gasbags inside her huge frame, that provided her lifting power, gigantic peas in a mammoth silvery pod, could not have been accommodated in the entire length of Westminster Abbey. Just one of these great gasbags had more lifting power than the entire total lift of the Italian airship, Norge, which had crossed the North Pole with Amundsen four years previously. The British airship R.33, which had been reconditioned as a prototype for R.101, could have flown through one of the rings that supported the girders in her waist as easily as a dog might jump through a circus hoop. Nothing so large, so complex and so expensive had ever flown before.

Even the mooring masts or towers that had been built at Cardington, Ismailia and Karachi to moor her were on a comparable scale. Each was higher than Nelson's Column and their complicated equipment included a lift, searchlights, a spiral staircase, and winches to pull in the airship as she came up to moor. These winches were housed in a machine house at the bottom of the mast and were operated by remote control from the masthead. An underground fuel tank capable of holding 10,000 gallons of fuel was alongside, with a pump which could raise 2,000 gallons an hour to a height of 400 feet - twice as high as was in fact required. Two other pumps pumped ballast water to the airship, at the rate of 5,000 gallons an hour. Gas was supplied to the bags through a twelve-inch gas main which ran up the tower. The tower itself 200 feet high and 70 feet across at its base, could take a pull at its top of 30 tons in any direction. The lift opened out on to a top platform, which was 40 feet across, and above this still was the conical turret which contained the tower head and its machinery.

Each of these towers had cost more than £50,000 to construct, and like the airship which would use them, they bristled with new ideas, including a means of rotating the top, designed by Major Scott, so that R. 101 at anchor could turn with the wind as a ship at anchor turns with the tide. This was an important development, for if airships were sometimes difficult to control in flight, because of their size and the enormous area they presented to the wind, they were many times more difficult to land. During the war they had operated from sheds, and to take an airship out of her shed, or to replace her after a flight was a hazardous performance that required a landing party of anything up to 300 men who would hold on to ropes dangling from her sides and 'walk' her out or in. When an airship arrived at her station unexpectedly, lorries were sent racing round the countryside to bring in servicemen and civilians for this purpose, and once in she could only be brought out again in suitable weather - for a crosswind would either dash her against the side of the shed or blow her away altogether.

If any sort of regular airship service was to be organized, then clearly one of the first essentials was an out-of-doors mooring mast, where she could ride in the sky, as a ship at anchor does in harbour, regardless of the weather. As an experiment, the airship R.24 was left riding at a mooring tower at Pulham for three weeks in 1919, and she survived high winds and rain. Attempts to land her by rope, however, were not very successful. The method of hauling in on a horizontal, or nearly horizontal, path by a single rope was both difficult and risky and led to 'surging' as she approached the tower. A new system was therefore tried out two years later with much greater success, and this was the means chosen for mooring R. 100 and R. 101. It was basically a simple idea: at the top of the tower a vertical receiving arm could swing through an angle of 30 degrees and so follow an airship's movements as she arrived and as the wind might move her when she was at anchor. The mooring wire attached to the steel cone on the airship's bow ran through the centre of this arm. Once the ship was hauled in, this bow was locked automatically into the receiving cup at the top of the arm. Surging upwards and yawing from side to side were prevented by two side guy ropes that stretched from the airship's nose to anchor blocks on the ground, 750 feet away from the tower.

When an airship was ready to land she first approached the tower upwind, at a height of between 600 and 1,000 feet; then the main wire was thrown out and the ground staff secured it to the tower wire, which had been reeled out until it also reached the ground. Winches then wound the airship into the mast. There was only one danger to the men who joined these two wires on the ground - the possibility of shock from static electricity which the airship line might have picked up in the sky. For this reason, the airship wire always touched the ground before anyone began to connect it to the other wire from the mooring mast. Once, as R. 101 came in to land at Cardington, a youngster on the ground staff, knowing nothing of this procedure, began to prance about, trying to catch the dangling wire as it was lowered from the airship. The tower commander saw his danger from the top of the mast and shouted to him but, owing to the noise of the engines, he could not be heard. Fortunately a rigger, who was on the ground, also realized the danger. He jumped on to a tractor, drove it out across the field towards the approaching airship, leapt from the driving seat and knocked the young fellow down with a single punch, an act that almost certainly saved his life.

The spirit of the R. 101 enterprise had been summarized shortly after work began on the building of the airship by Sir Samuel Hoare, then Secretary of State for Air, at the Lord Mayor's Banquet in London. He said: 'We hope to be able to show by the experiments upon which we have now embarked in connection with the development of airships that, in the course of a few years, it will be as possible to have a regular airship service between London and Bombay as it is now to have an aeroplane service between London and Paris.'

In the 1920s, when aeroplanes were still small and relatively unreliable, it was widely believed that the future of long-distance air travel lay with airships which could soar through the air, secure in the gas that supported them, and in their own great size. In 1919, Alcock and Brown had flown an aeroplane across the Atlantic for the first time, but no aeroplane had yet flown that journey with a paying passenger, although airships had made several crossings. Passenger flights in trans-Atlantic aeroplanes remained something of a novelty until the Second World War. The first regular trans-Atlantic aeroplane service was started in 1939 by Pan American Airways, and it was not until the following year, when the war situation demanded desperate measures, that aircraft regularly flew the Atlantic in winter.

Alcock and Brown, flying from west to east, had wisely kept the prevailing wind behind them, but in 1930 an aeroplane had still to fly against this wind from England to America. The airship R.34, however, had made the crossing both ways in 1919, and so much did the Admiralty regard the trip as a matter of routine that, with an all-too-British disregard for the value of publicity, they actually waited until Alcock and Brown had crossed in June before allowing their airship to set out in the following month. Then R.34, one of the most successful airships ever built in Britain, set out with six officers, a crew of twenty, one stowaway and 40 lb of mail, and flew from Scotland to America and back again without any trouble at all.

The idea that aeroplanes would ever be able to carry anything like as many passengers on such a journey was not held to be practical. Such things might come to pass in time, but there would be years yet in which airships could establish their superiority as carriers of passengers and freight over long distances, while aeroplanes were more suitable for short hops within the boundaries of the country. An aeroplane could average 120 mph by day and would not fly on a long journey through the night. An airship, on the other hand, could keep up an average of 60 mph by day and night. Looked at from this angle, airships seemed to compete on equal terms with aeroplanes, over long distances.

That this belief should persist in view of such successful and well-publicized flights as that of Sir Samuel and Lady Maud Hoare to India in 1925, and Amy Johnson's solo flight from England to Australia shortly before R.101 set out for Egypt, shows how lightly the aeroplane was regarded. It was a clever toy, an amazing flying machine, but not to be considered in the same breath as a rival to the established ways of travel, by sea and by rail. Some, like Sir Sefton Brancker, believed that the future held great things for the flying boat; others felt that the aeroplane had already reached the limit of technical achievement. One subscriber to this theory published a book on airships towards the end of 1930 in which he forecast possible trends in aviation.

'Already,' he declared, 'we are beginning to probe the boundaries of commercial aeroplane performance in certain respects... Popular writers are addicted to preparing a diagram, termed a "graph", indicating (say) the rise of the maximum speed of aeroplanes from some 40 mph in 1909 to some 350 mph in 1930.

'Continuing the curve upwards they show that in 1950 aircraft will be capable of (say) 700 mph. Such diagrams are, of course, no more graphs exhibiting a true function than are temperature charts, and it might be almost as legitimate to assume that, because a fever patient's chart showed a rise of 4 degrees from March 1st to March 8th, 1930, then in 1935 his blood would be boiling."

This strange reasoning even coloured official decisions. Had the speed of passenger-carrying aeroplanes been faster in 1924 then the airship's proposed cruising speed of about 63 miles an hour (which it never in fact maintained) would have been absurd. Today, this is barely the cruising speed of a family car, but in 1924, compared with the speed of the fastest liner - the *Mauretania* - and thinking was still on a basis of air-to-sea comparison, it was considered a wonderful thing, for the history of lighter-than-air flight went back a long way, although until fairly recent times Britain had contributed very little to it.

The French were the pioneers, a century and a half earlier, and Germany, seeing a military value in airships, had developed the idea to a remarkable extent while the British Government was still only allowing a very small budget for research, and this most grudgingly given. The military authorities could see no use for an air arm, and the Navy were jealous of their position as Britain's senior service. And, as Dr Eckener, the German airship pioneer and designer of the Graf Zeppelin, said in a lecture he gave in the Scala Theatre, London, during the construction of R.101: 'In this most perfect world, you can't get any government money unless the apparatus has a potential value in war.'

The first flight of a lighter-than-air machine took place 147 years before the airship R.101 left England for Egypt - in the spring of 1783, when Joseph and Stephen Montgolfier, the sons of a French paper-maker, sitting by their fire at Annonay, on a winter evening, began to wonder why smoke should always rise. They decided to discover whether it could be made to raise something in it, and they built a paper sphere 35 feet in diameter, and hung under this a brazier of glowing charcoal. The hot air rose from the brazier and bore the balloon up into the sky. The French Academy of Science, impressed by this performance, asked them to repeat it in Paris before a wider audience. While they were building a second balloon for the purpose, however, a French physicist, Professor J A C Charles, built a balloon himself; filled it with hydrogen, and flew it in August. To be beaten by a Parisian annoyed the elder Montgolfier, and he determined that his balloon would at least be the first to carry passengers. So, when the Montgolfier brothers let loose their second hot-air balloon from the grounds of the Palace of Versailles, before Louis XVI, it supported a gondola containing a sheep, a duck and a cock.[2]

In October they decided to send a balloon aloft with human passengers. Later aeronauts, like Colonel Richmond in the R.101, flew in the airships they had themselves designed, but no volunteers seemed likely for this first passenger flight. A judge solved the problem by offering to a group of criminals (who would otherwise be executed) the choice of volunteering for an aerial journey. Two stepped forward; the balloon trip at least offered a chance of survival.

A young courtier, Jean Philatre de Rozier, felt that the occasion was one for panache, and not to be thrown away on reluctant felons.

'The honour of being the first man to fly should not go to a convict, but to a gentleman of France,' he announced. 'I offer my life.'

The offer was accepted, and so to the cheers of thousands of Parisians he became airborne on November 21, 1783, flew halfway across Paris and landed safely, having by this brief journey ensured that his name survived the centuries. One of the spectators of this flight was Benjamin Franklin, the American Ambassador, and a scientist of renown, who even then believed that aeronautics would become important.

'But of what *use* is a balloon?' someone asked him sceptically.

'Of what use,' retorted Franklin, 'is a newborn baby?'

The last element of the air was thus under attack, but lighter-than-air vessels seemed unusually prone to humiliating accidents. In the following year, for instance, two other French brothers, the Roberts, designed for the Due de Chartres an airship to look like a fish, on the reasonable theory that if a fish could swim in water then a fish-shape would acquit itself well in the sky. This flying fish, 52 feet long, had a capacity of 30,000 cubic feet and was 'rowed' along with oars six feet across. Unfortunately, no gas could be let out during the flight, for the brothers had carefully designed it with a double envelope to prevent leakage, and the whole balloon would have burst on its first flight had not the Due, as chief passenger, seen the danger, and resourcefully rammed a flagstaff through the envelope to let the expanding gas go free. As a result, they came down gently and ignominiously to earth, with nothing lost but their pride.

A contemporary account[3] of a further flight in France that year deserves quoting at length for it shows in microcosm the ills that dogged so many subsequent airship ventures: the wish of the public for a spectacle conflicting with the natural caution of those who were to fly in the aerial ship; the strength of will against the weakness of the machine they had created.

The people shouted and huzzaed from every quarter. A great number of mortars were let off, and at last the gas being introduced into the machine, we saw it majestically rising... The gallery began to rise two feet, but as it was too late to trust it to any height, the sport, or rather the spectacle was put off till the subsequent day.

'On Friday, all the provisions being ready, the travellers, to the number of six, got up into the gallery, hankering after the moment of the departure, which was at last announced by the discharge of several mortars. M. Durofier putting now in the hands of M. Montgolfier some straw and some fire, the latter carried the same in triumph to M. de Fleffelle, the Intendant; this produced a general peal of endless acclamations, bravos, and huzzas.

The fire was put, but the unfortunate machine had hardly gained the height of fifty feet, when the top catched fire, which, however, was soon extinguished by engines; but the machine fell down in a very sad condition. It was found necessary to change all the superior part, and a portion of the segment, so that it was absolutely impossible for it to go off. The disappointment occasioned many long faces. MM. Durofier and Montgolfier had tears in their eyes: the public went away not well pleased.

'At first a violent fire was made under it, contrary to the orders of M. Durofier; the machine being loaded with damp articles, acquired a great degree of heaviness, and was sinking fast on the flame. A great number of people, however, actuated by a kind of enthusiasm, gave every sort of assistance in their power; and, in spite of the wind, the rain, and the snow, for all the elements seemed to conspire against that unlucky machine, the whole was at last repaired, and the departure fixed for this day, the 19th, at ten o'clock in the morning. The crowd, as I said before, was prodigious.

The operation now began: it is impossible to describe, at this time, the anxiety of the people; their minds seemed to fluctuate between hope and fear; the machine started with a great deal of majesty, assuming the best form that could be wished; it was soon filled up, and nothing wanting for its going off but the signal of the captain M. Durofier. Here a most extraordinary scene ensued. M. Durofier, considering the indifferent condition of the machine, that had greatly suffered from various trials, assured that the experiment must certainly fail, if more than three persons embarked.

'But those who had placed themselves in the gallery would not listen to him; and being all armed with pistols, declared that sooner than descend they would blow their own brains out. Upon which Messrs. Durofier and Montgolfier applied to M. Fleffelle, the Intendant, requesting him to interpose his authority, and to make them draw lots. He accordingly came near the gallery, and endeavoured to persuade them into the measure that had been suggested to him, but every one of the travellers pretended to have a certain right to remain where he was, and would by no means trust to chance the glory of travelling in such a splendid aerial equipage.

'Finding that their obstinacy was unconquerable, M. Philatre gave the signal with some regret. The ropes, however, being cut off, the machine gained a high elevation, and followed for some time an horizontal direction, crossing our heads in the enclosure. The people appeared extremely uneasy, especially the women, who were all in tears. The aerial travellers, however, showed themselves full of confidence, moving their hats out of the gallery and shouting for ever. The wind happening to shift, the machine immediately rose towards Dauphine with the greatest rapidity, which filled every spectator with a kind of extatic joy, enhanced by the sound of martial instruments, and the discharge of a number of mortars; but our happiness did not last long. The machine having reached the height of four hundred toises, so that it appeared to us as a balloon of about ten or twelve feet in circumference, it began to sink, and when it came to but one hundred toises, it descended with such celerity, that in an instant we saw it on the ground.

'No less than sixty thousand people, besides the Marech-aussee, ran to the spot with the greatest apprehension for the lives of those unfortunate aerial travellers. Luckily none of them had received any hurt, except M. Montgolfier an insignificant scratch. The cause of their ill-success was owing to a little rent accidentally happening in the interior part of the machine, and which soon enlarging itself, made room for a considerable portion of atmospherical air, a circumstance that rendered the fall of the machine inevitable.

There was, besides, a young man called Fontaine, nephew to a Madame Fontaine, who had superintended all the dressing of the machine. It is worth observing that this young man had been promised a place in the gallery, and then had been excluded. As he was determined not to be disappointed, he watched the moment the machine crossed the enclosure, and jumped into the gallery. When the other travellers had attained a certain height, they were surprised to find the young man among them, and were beginning to express their indignation, when he told them with the greatest composure, that on earth he would certainly respect their orders, but the place he was then in authorised him to think himself equal to them.

'M. Philatre rode home on horseback, and such was the popular enthusiasm, that every one disputed the honour of holding the bridle of his horse...'

More practical balloons were used for military observations in the French Revolution and the American Civil War. In 1851, the year of the Great Exhibition, another Frenchman, Henri Giffard (also the inventor of the steam injector) powered an airship with a three-horsepower steam engine, which turned an 11 foot propeller at 110 revolutions per minute. With this engine installed in a 114-foot hydrogen-filled airship he made an ascent from the Hippodrome in Paris and travelled at six miles an hour, apparently unconcerned about the fearful consequences that could have arisen had the wind blown flames from his engine too close to the gas envelope. Twelve years later a Viennese, Paul Haenlein, flew an airship driven by gas engine, and then two more French brothers, Albert and Gaston Tissandier, flew the first electrically powered airship. The problem of motive power was within sight of solution, but a much bigger one remained - and indeed, was never solved satisfactorily: that of complete control while in the air, for a flying machine of such enormous and unwieldy size as an airship was perpetually at the mercy of the winds. Even with the later British designs, a strong wind could drive them out to sea. Just before her trip to America in 1919, the R.34 encountered a gale over the North Sea, and although at full throttle and travelling through the air at 40 knots, was actually blown astern for eight hours!

Again, during a gale in April, 1925, the mooring arm holding the R.33 suddenly snapped, and she was driven on to the mast, which crushed in her bows and punctured the No. 1 gasbag. Then the wind changed and blew her out over the North Sea towards the Dutch Coast. Flight-Lieutenant Irwin's deputy, Flight-Lieutenant Ralph Booth, who later took over R.100, was on duty. He brought her back to England in twenty-nine and a half hours, travelling in reverse all the way. That the R.33 returned at all was due to the bravery of all aboard her, and to his brilliant handling. But it was perhaps surprising that Major G H Scott, who was then commanding Pulham Air Station, described it as 'one of the greatest achievements in airships in Britain, America or Germany'; it added nothing to public confidence in the reliability of British airships, for she should not have blown away in the first place.

'Almost a year to the day after the R.33 excitement,' wrote Sir Samuel Hoare[4] (then Air Minister), 'I was once more at Pulham to welcome an Italian airship under the command of Colonel Nobile.

The airship, financed by Mussolini, a group of American journalists and Amundsen, the Arctic explorer, was on its way to the North Pole.

'Colonel Nobile was timed to arrive at ten am, but we saw nothing of the airship until late afternoon. At last, the airship came in sight, and we thought that our hours of waiting and watching had at last ended. But to our dismay, there were still two or three more hours before the airship condescended to land. In the meanwhile, she circled round and made repeated movements as if she were landing. Then she would suddenly rise and go through the same tantalizing procedure. When she finally came down and was with immense difficulty pulled into a shed by over a hundred agricultural labourers, Captain G H Scott, our expert navigator, who had joined the flight in Rome, came across to me and told me that he could not have had a more uncomfortable voyage. The cold had been intense as someone had broken a window before they started; there was only room for two of the passengers to sit down at a time and the Italians, Norwegians and Americans could not understand each others' language and never ceased quarrelling. Finally, Colonel Nobile had a *crise de nerfs,* and every time the airship was about to land, had insisted upon ballast being thrown out for fear of crashing on the ground, with the result that the airship bounded up again like a tennis ball...'

So dependent on wind and weather were all airships, that when the meteorological conditions of the proposed Empire airship routes came to be calculated, the 'roaring forties' of the windjammer days were thought to have a further important part to play. The Empire had been opened up by pioneers in sailing ships, and since the new pioneers of the 1930s would sail to these same Empire countries in airships, the winds that blew their forefathers would also help them on their way.

All these rigid airships were controlled by a system of tailplanes, like vertical and horizontal rudders, that were fixed to the rigid skeleton of the vessel. The fact that any rigid airships were built at all was due to a German, David Schwarz, who made the first in 1897, using an aluminium frame and cover to minimize the dangers of gas leakage. He was also the first man to use a petrol engine as his motive power, but, like many other airships, his invention had a brief and unfortunate career. On her first trial she met a headwind of 16 miles an hour which forced him to run his engine at full throttle. This broke a belt that drove the propeller, and the whole contraption came down to earth where a crowd, who had gathered to watch, felt that they were being cheated out of a better demonstration and so fell on the disabled airship and completely wrecked her.

In 1900 petrol finally ousted steam or electricity as a lighter and less clumsy method of propulsion, and progress began to be made, with Germany leading. Graf Ferdinand von Zeppelin, an officer in the German Army, became so enamoured of the idea of developing airships that he retired from the Army to devote himself to them and designed an entirely new rigid type, shaped like a pencil, with a covering of waterproof cotton cloth stretched over an aluminium framework of sixteen hoops, all rigidly connected by wire stays. This first Zeppelin was divided by transverse aluminium frames into seventeen gas compartments - one more than the R. 101 originally possessed. A latticed keel ran beneath the vessel with an external car containing a 16-horsepower engine geared to two propellers towards the front and rear of the airship. She could be raised or lowered by moving a sliding weight along the keel.

Count Zeppelin had many setbacks, both financial and technical, but so basically successful was his experiment that his enthusiasm received both public and Government support, and a fund was opened on his account which realized £300,000. With this he began to build an airship works at Freidrichshafen, and during the next fourteen years no less than twenty-five Zeppelins were built and flown with dogged enthusiasm and much success. The German Army had faith in them, and by the outbreak of the First World War they were using six rigid Zeppelins and three other airships; by the end, they were operating eighty-eight Zeppelins which were being built at four factories. Some of these German airships silently drifted over England towards London during the war at something like 20,000 feet, where the cold was so intense that engines stalled and could not be restarted. Sometimes members of the crew were lowered on long ropes through the clouds in a desperate attempt to spot a landmark. Many of these lookouts died as a result of being lowered through clouds that were charged with static electricity.

Under the Treaty of Versailles, all. building ceased in Germany, and the existing airships were turned over to the Allies as reparations. One was renamed the *Los Angeles,* and travelled to America where she lasted until 1932, when she was broken up. Another, called the *Dixmude,* was claimed by France and went down over the Mediterranean in 1923 with the loss of all aboard her. The British used captured Zeppelins as models for craft of their own, which were almost slavish copies of their originals, for such airships as were being constructed in Britain were built by empirical methods and by men used to constructing Navy vessels. They therefore made their airships strong enough to bear their loads under static conditions, but without any knowledge at all of the fearful aerodynamic problems that a vessel two hundreds yards long can present when it meets with uncharted and unpredictable air currents. This was shown in the 1920s when a German officer arrived at Pulham on a courtesy visit and was shown a British airship that had been diligently copied, girder by girder, from a wartime German design. Courtesy kept him silent as he was shown over this strange production, but at last he allowed himself one comment.

'Splendid, splendid,' he said without enthusiasm. 'You have copied us - *even to our mistakes.'*

Within a few years, German interest in lighter-than-air craft was again being given free rein, and in 1928 they completed the famous *Graf Zeppelin,* which flew for nine years and covered more than a million miles of passenger and mail flights between Europe and America. The United States preferred privately-owned and -built airships, which they started to produce early in the century, but they also had setbacks; the American Navy operated the *Shenandoah,* which like the British airships, was largely based on Zeppelin design, and although she made a transcontinental trip of 9,000 miles, because she was filled with the non-inflammable and very expensive helium gas, her gas-escape valves - which were in any case small for the size of the ship - were tightened down. During a storm over Ohio she met with i a sudden upward gust of wind and the valves could not cope with the volume of gas that had to go free. As a result she broke up in the air.

In Germany and America airship progress stemmed from an enthusiasm which overrode all disasters, and a natural willingness to spend money on experiment and trials. In Britain, the story was different. The amount of money that successive governments could be persuaded to pay for research and experiment was very small, for they were chary of spending either time or money on so ephemeral an aim as the conquest of the air. In the early years of the century an official report on aerial research gave the reason for this reluctance. It declared that 'the policy of the Government with regard to all branches of aerial navigation is based on a desire to keep in touch with the movement rather than to hasten its development. It is felt that we stand to gain nothing by forcing a means of warfare which tends to reduce the value of our insular position and the protection of our sea power.

This official attitude was no new thing, for as long ago as 1804 similar thinking had prevented Rear-Admiral Earl St Vincent taking advantage of an offer by an American inventor, Robert Fulton, to build a submarine, on the grounds that if Britain pursued such researches, then so would other countries, a state of affairs the Admiral felt that would 'become the greatest blow at our supremacy on the sea that can be imagined.'

Similarly, despite advances made by other countries in the design of dirigible airships, it was not until 1902 that Colonel Templer, then in charge of the Army Ballooning Department of the War Office, persuaded his superiors that he should be allotted enough money to build an airship. He was only allowed enough to build two envelopes of goldbeater's skin of 50,000 cubic feet apiece, but five years later, his successor, Colonel J E Capper, received permission to build the first British military airship, the *Nulli Secundus,* using for economy one of Colonel Templer's original envelopes. This airship was 120 feet long, powered by a 40-horsepower Antoinette engine, driving two propellers with metal blades, and she flew from Farnborough to London at 16 miles an hour, circled round Buckingham Palace and St Paul's and set off on the return journey. Her speed on the way to the capital owed much to a following wind, against which the aviators could make no progress on their way back, and finally they were forced to land on the cycling track at Crystal Palace, deflate their balloon, and return to Farnborough by road.

Two years later, the second British military airship was built, the *Baby,* so called because she had a capacity of only 21,000 cubic feet. Initially she was not very satisfactory, and so she was enlarged and fitted with a more powerful engine - an attempt at overcoming initial errors very popular with airship designers, and based apparently on the belief that what was bigger must also be better. This thinking also prevailed with R.101, which, as we have seen, was lengthened - by 45 feet - shortly before she set off for Egypt.

The *Baby* was renamed the *Beta,* and flew from Farnborough to London and back again one night in four hours, the first night flight made by a British airship. She further distinguished herself by carrying three men and six homing pigeons - a form of communication which found much favour with the Army -at 37 miles an hour. Her elevators were small and badly placed, however, and each ascent and descent was frightening to watch and even worse to endure.

The Navy had also become interested in airships, and the Committee of Imperial Defence persuaded the Treasury to allow £35,000 to be spent on a rigid naval airship to be known as His Majesty's Airship No.1 and capable of being moored on water. In shape like a pencil, 512 feet long and pointed at both ends, this airship was powered by two Wolseley engines of 200 horsepower. Work began on her in May 1909, in a special shed at Cavendish Dock, Barrow-in-Furness, by Vickers, who were later to build the successful R. 100. She came out for her trials exactly two years later (and at a final cost of £100,000), but seemed so heavy that cynics, doubting whether she would ever fly, were not surprised when she was christened the *Mayfly.* She fully justified these prophecies and broke in two as she was being taken out of her gigantic shed with her nose over the water, and began to sink. Officers and crew had to jump and swim for their lives. She never flew at all and her loss drew some sharp comments from others who favoured aeroplanes instead of airships. Robert Loraine, the famous actor-aviator of the day, declared that it was 'only what everybody had been expecting. The whole history of the machine has been a chapter of accidents,' he declared. 'Why the authorities persist in these experiments with dirigibles is a mystery to me. There has not been a single test in recent years in which the aeroplane's superiority has not been constantly apparent...'

If the airship was wasted, at least her shed was not, for during the early part of the First War, when the Navy wanted airships quickly for submarine patrol work, it was decided to build a large rigid airship. Then officials found that there was no shed in the country large enough to house such a monster, and work started at once to build one. Only half the girders were set in position when the Steel Commission refused to let the builders have any more steel to finish the job, and as an alternative, it was suggested that the Vickers shed, which had been used for the *Mayfly,* should again be used. Thus, the new airship was designed to fit a shed more than the task in hand and was obsolete before she was begun.

After the *Mayfly* fiasco the Naval Airship Section was disbanded, but was reformed in August 1913 as No.1 squadron, Royal Flying Corps, stationed at Farnborough. Major G M Maitland, one of the great aeronautical enthusiasts of the age, was in command, and he demonstrated how radio could be used to communicate from air to land - as opposed to the older way of using homing pigeons, or simply wrapping a message form round a spanner and dropping it over the side.

Then in January 1914 airships were transferred back to Navy control.

Sir Sefton Brancker[5] described the transfer thus in his diary: 'During 1913, in their attitude towards aviation, Winston Churchill (First Lord of the Admiralty) and Seely (Secretary of State for War) might be compared to a pair of light-hearted schoolboys who had each been given a new pony!... They used to meet during weekends, and decide questions of aerial policy without referring to anyone... Quite suddenly one morning Colonel Seely wrote a minute on War Office paper in his own handwriting announcing that the First Lord and he had decided to transfer the whole of the military airships to the Navy Wing...' Officers and crews of British airships wore naval-type uniforms, crews had the number of their airship in their cap badges.

During and after the war, a number of airships were built at Government expense and under Government direction. Some were based, like R.33 and R.34, on captured German craft. Others were less successful: the R.35, for instance, cost nearly £75,000 but was never completed. The R.36 was built as a passenger ship at a cost of £350,000, met with an accident two months after launching, was partially reconditioned for £13,500, but never flew again. Nearly £325,000 was spent on her successor, the R.37, until the design was abandoned. Then came disaster with R.38, a wartime design and intended for service over the North Sea, which meant that she needed the unusually high ceiling of 25,000 feet, quite unnecessary for civilian use.

She had been begun in 1918 but after the war it was intended that she should be sold to the United States after her initial trial flights. She was to be 699 feet long and it was stipulated that she was to be built at the existing sheds at Cardington, but as things turned out this meant that there was insufficient space for her naval constructors to produce a really good design.

'In the construction of such an airship,' reported a Commission which sat in 1921 to inquire into her loss, 'it was not sufficient to place exclusive reliance on a comparison with existing ships using the routine methods adopted for R.38.' The intention was to produce a ship with structural stresses no greater than those of earlier airships, but the calculations did not allow for movement under differing air pressures, and were based throughout on an assumption of static conditions, which, of course, an aircraft never meets unless on the ground. The designers had seen for themselves how the pressure distributed round a model airship showed bending movements to a high degree, yet throughout they regarded the aerodynamic stresses as being less important than the static. Nor was any outside opinion asked on the stress calculations of the ship, although such data was available had the Advisory Committee for Aeronautics been consulted.

The aerodynamic stresses she would meet were far greater than with R.33, and yet her safety factor in flight was only half that of the earlier, smaller airship. She made four trial flights, and each showed new weaknesses. First her rudders and elevators were found to be overbalanced; then the control wires were too slack to allow for control above the speed of 38 knots, finally the fins proved to be structurally weak and had to be strengthened.

At last, on 23 August 1921, with G M Maitland, by now an Air Commodore, and a crack British crew aboard, plus an American crew who were to fly her back to the States, she set off for her trial flight over the Humber. The weather was foggy, but by four-thirty on the following afternoon conditions had improved and she was able to signal her intention of going on to full speed. She reached a speed of 60 knots and then slowed for rudder trials. Her helm was put hard-a-starboard and then hard-a-port several times in quick succession, a performance that would break the back of many a naval destroyer, and spectators on the ground below saw a slackness in the fabric between two of her girders and realized that the structure inside must have collapsed under the strain.

Within seconds she broke in two. The forward half burst at once into flames, and fell into the river; the rear half fell comparatively slowly and did not take fire. Only five survived out of a total of forty-nine, and Air Commodore Maitland, the most brilliant airship officer in the country, was among the dead.

After this fiasco no one was surprised that although nearly £90,000 had been spent on the next airship, R.39, the contract was cancelled. The incident had nevertheless one worthwhile outcome, for it resulted in the setting up of two committees to consider the stresses and strains that airships could meet in flight, and other matters connected with them. The first, over which Professor (now Sir) Richard Southwell presided, was called "The Airship Stressing Panel' and the second, headed by Professor (now Sir) Leonard Bairstow was known as 'The Airworthiness of Airships Panel'. The factors of safety agreed by this latter panel were to be taken as the basis for certifying the airworthiness of the greatest airship of all, R.101.

In view of these disasters plenty of critics reminded others, more sanguine, of what happened to British airships, and plenty of prophets foretold worse things. One of the most vocal was Mr F H Rose, a former wheelwright and patternmaker, who had also been a trades union official, a journalist and a writer of plays. As the Socialist Member for North Aberdeen he showed his value as a prophet by declaring in a speech in his constituency that the 'heavier-than-air machine has no future at all, except as an instrument of war', and having thus summarily disposed of the aeroplane, he turned his attention to the future of the airship.

'I have never been up in an airship,' he went on, 'and have no intention of doing so. So far as my influence extends, airships will never be used. I do not know whence passengers for new airships are to be found. Colney Hatch has been suggested, but I think Broadmoor would be better... Man will never override natural laws, and it is because airships are a defiance of natural laws that I do not like them...'

In 1928, when work on the two great airships, R.100 and R.101, was well advanced, Sir Samuel Hoare, in presenting the Air Estimates in the House of Commons, asked for a further £100,000 more than it had been anticipated would be spent on them. This gave Mr Rose his chance.

'Let us see what we have done since the war in this connection,' he began, 'and remember that all the talent and all the virtues of the Air Minister have been brought to bear on these subjects.

'R.33 cost £350,000, and she flew for 800 hours and burst. R.34 cost £350,000 and burst. R.35 cost £75,000 and burst before she was inflated. R.36 cost £350,000, flew for 97 hours, and burst. R.37 cost £325,000 and was never completed. R.38 cost £500,000. She was built at Cardington, and they always charge more at Cardington, and she flew for 70 hours and burst. R.39 cost £90,000 and was never finished. She was scrapped and used as a stress test. R.40 cost £275,000, flew for 73 hours and burst. The total for eight ships is £2,315,000, and the total flying time 1,540 hours.' Mr Rose went on to quote estimates for expenditure on the R.101, which would be '£229,000 on material, £65,000 on shop labour, £35,000 on drawing office labour...and £80,000 for overhead charges. That is a total for the airship itself of £409,000...

"Then there is the power plant chargeable to this particular ship, which amounts to £35,000. In addition two engines which were made for experimental purposes are going to be utilized and their value is assessed at £16,000, making a total of £460,000 for a ship which has hardly been begun, which has been in hand now for four years, but cannot, by any possibility, take the air this year if it does so next year or ever. Thus £460,000 of the taxpayers' money has gone or will go in this scheme...'

It is against this strange patchwork background of inconclusive tests, unfortunate accidents, genuine belief in airships and downright ignorance that the Government finally decided, in 1924, to take an interest in them. But, as with so many other enterprises with which the State has been associated, the interest was too little and came too late; and when this was finally realized, results were wanted far too soon.

1. Christopher Sprigg, *The Airship* (Hutchinson).

2. These airborne animals were not forgotten. Years later, when the US Army Corps cast about for a badge for its lighter-than-air division, the final design included a sheep, a duck and a cock.

3. From *The London Magazine,* February 1784.

4. Viscount Templewood (Sir Samuel Hoare), *Empire of the Air* (Collins).

5. Norman MacMillan: *Sefton Brancker* (Heinemann).

CHAPTER THREE
The Length, the Breadth and the Height

That the British Government became interested in airships and an airship service at all, even at such a late hour, was mainly due to the vision and enthusiasm of Commander (later Sir) Dennistoun Burney, a man whose prodigious inventive power was only equalled by his enthusiasm for whatever project he had in hand, whether it was the paravane anti-submarine device of the First War, the Burney Streamline car, or a revolutionary way of building prefabricated houses.

All his ideas were unique in being far ahead of their time and bearing the mark of genius. The Burney Streamline car, for instance, which he began to sell only the month before R.101 left Cardington, had a rear engine and independent suspension on all wheels - innovations that are still regarded in this country as being unorthodox and advanced. The Prince of Wales, now the Duke of Windsor, drove one of the first, and George Ladbrook, his chauffeur for eighteen years, still speaks of it with affection. 'It was delightful to drive,' he says. 'A tremendous amount of thought had gone into it.'

This quality characterized all Burney's inventions, nor have his powers diminished with the years, for during the Second World War he worked on a scheme to have small fighter aeroplanes attached to a larger parent aircraft - as planes had flown years previously from the airship R.33 - and also did valuable pioneering work on the development of recoilless guns. And since the war he has interested himself in new means of catching and freezing fish on a vast scale - and even ventured into theatrical management.

Dennistoun Burney was the son of Admiral Sir Cecil Burney, who had been Lord Jellicoe's Second-in-Command at Jutland and afterwards Second Sea Lord. He shared his father's interest in engineering and the sea, and entered the Navy as a cadet in 1903. Only six years later he decided that the provision of effective weapons of offence against submarines was essential for the future survival of the Navy, and accordingly went on half pay so that he could develop a type of seaplane which could drop depth charges. In 1911 he was appointed to HMS *Excellent,* and produced various anti-submarine devices such as the automatic depth recorder, and the single sweep hydroplane. Inventions soon began to take up so much of his thoughts that he again applied for half pay, so that he could develop a seaplane. The design seemed on the point of success when war broke out. This gave him the opportunity to develop the inventions that made him famous, the explosive paravane and the protector paravane. The first was used to destroy submarines and the second as a means of protecting ships from mines. Basically - and an airship possesses certain qualities in common with a submarine - the paravane was a water kite, which was towed by a ship. This made it run outwards and downwards, and in so doing it cut the moorings of the mines. The Lords of the Admiralty could not believe that such a seemingly simple design could be successful, but Burney was proved right, for during the war his invention saved an estimated £100,000,000 worth of shipping. The Admiralty allowed him to dispose of certain rights in this invention on his own behalf, and this earned him £265,000. Three years afterwards he resigned from the Navy and became Conservative MP for Uxbridge, a constituency he represented until he resigned in 1929 to spend more time on the problem of lighter-than-air craft, in which his interest had been growing for some years. Shortly after he became an MP preparations were announced to transfer various obsolete airships to the Disposals Board for breaking up or for sale, in the unlikely hope of customers being found. Burney considered this a gross waste, for the total cost of their manufacture ran into hundreds of thousands of pounds, and much had been learned from them. He proposed that a regular airship service for passengers, goods and mail should be organized between London and the main cities of the Empire, and drew attention to the economic, political and strategic advantages which could be expected to result.

In the first instance, he suggested there should be a giant airship, much larger than the R.33, which could fly to India by way of Egypt in 74 hours (an enormous improvement on the 17 days needed for a sea voyage) and gradually, as the service progressed, other airships would be constructed until a fleet of six were each carrying 10 tons of mail and between 130 and 150 passengers twice a week to India. The fare would be between £70 and £80, which was rather less than that charged by P&O liners of the time. Both the Shell and Vickers concerns were interested in promoting this service, and Burney propounded its immense Imperial significance with great vigour within Parliament and without.

These airships would fly the aerial routes just as, beneath them, ships were sailing in the sea lanes. As he described it, the vision was calculated to stir the most apathetic heart, and the Conservative Government of the day agreed that it should be thoroughly examined. Indeed, nine government committees examined it, but the Government lost office before anything definite could be done to translate the dream into reality. And when the first Labour Government came in, under Ramsay MacDonald, they decided to review the whole state of affairs and so appointed a further Cabinet Committee for this purpose.

The Socialists did not feel that private firms should build all the airships, since they naturally wanted to show the superiority of State enterprise, so for some time they could reach no conclusion. Then, with that British delight in compromise which also provides a ready-made escape from the necessity of making an unpopular decision, the Cabinet Committee decided to favour neither side wholeheartedly. Instead, so that both private enterprise and the State should compete, the Royal Airship Works at Cardington would build one airship of a certain size and speed, and Vickers, under their offshoot, the Airship Guarantee Company Ltd., would build another of similar performance. Then the public would be able to see which produced the better airship: public or private enterprise.

A young engineer, Nevil Shute Norway, who was engaged as a calculator for the private enterprise airship, R.100, which would be constructed at Howden in Yorkshire, looked back on this decision years afterwards when he was more widely known as Nevil Shute, the novelist.

'The controversy of capitalism versus State enterprise has been argued, tested and fought out in many ways in many countries,' he wrote, 'but surely the airship venture in England stands as the most curious determination of this matter."

The requirements for both airships were formidable, and far in advance of anything previously built to fly. Each would contain 5,000,000 cubic feet of hydrogen, which would give a gross lift of 150 tons - nearly twice as much as that possessed by any previous British airship, and more than a third as much again as the lift of the world's most successful airship, the Zeppelin.

The two new airships would have a maximum speed of 70 mph and be able to cruise at 63 mph, at which speed 100 passengers with first-class eating and sleeping accommodation could be carried through the sky. Neither airship was to weigh more than 90 tons, without fuel, and so the 'useful' lift - the weight of passengers, fuel and stores each airship could carry -would be 60 tons, roughly 40 per cent of the gross lift. A final condition laid it down that both airships would run on fuel that could safely be carried in the tropics, and, for the first time in British airship history, each ship would have to provide definite factors of safety, and proof that she could withstand aerodynamic forces, to a degree decided by the Aeronautical Research Committee. Designs were therefore prepared and approved and work began at Howden in Yorkshire, where the R. 100 was being built to the designs of Barnes Neville Wallis, one of the most brilliant and versatile engineers of the century, whose talents have ranged from designing aeroplanes such as the Wellington to the giant 'Dam Buster' bombs that breached the Moehne and the Eder Dams in the Second World War. The chief designer at Cardington was to be Colonel Vincent Richmond, who had studied airship technique in Germany and who now was determined to make R.101 the best airship ever built in Britain. Both teams were convinced that theirs was far superior to their rivals', and this spirit grew more bitter as time went on in a way that neither side wished but which they were powerless to prevent.

Soon the Conservatives were back in power, and Sir Samuel Hoare was Air Minister for the second time. 'Whilst there were plausible arguments in favour of competition between the State and private enterprise, there proved in practice to be an even stronger argument against it,' he wrote many years later. 'The number of experts who knew anything about airships could be counted on two hands... There were really not enough skilled men...to divide between two widely separated efforts of construction. There was the further disadvantage that the small and separated groups were apt to look with suspicion and sometimes jealousy at each other's work.'[2]

In 1926, however, when work had already been in progress for two years, Sir Samuel Hoare presumably felt more optimistic, for he prepared a memorandum for the Imperial Conference then being held in London, to help those with short memories who were beginning to wonder how and why the airship programme started, and when results could be expected.

He wrote that 'It was held that once this programme had been carried out the further development of airships could be assured, and it was recognized that the practical progress of the experimental programme might well prove to be of decisive importance in the history of airship development. It was, therefore, decided to develop the programme in a spirit of scientific caution, holding considerations of prudence and safety to be of paramount importance. Two airships were to be built, one by the Air Ministry (R.101) and one by the Airship Guarantee Company (R.100). This ensured competition in design and provided that a purely accidental failure of one ship should not terminate the whole programme.

'Elaborate researches and experiments were to be made; new sheds and masts were to be erected in England, Egypt and India; and the weather conditions of the route were to be carefully investigated in their application to airship navigation.'

In the eyes of the British public, at least, this policy had the elements of a sporting contest, and therefore must be good. And, at the beginning, no one thought of difficulties. Later, they argued quite loudly for themselves.

The news of this programme was naturally hailed with delight in Bedford for, at Cardington, what had been a wartime airship base of some size had been whittled down by the economies of successive governments to an airfield with some airship sheds existing on little more than a care and maintenance basis. There was also much unemployment in the area; Shortstown, a village built originally to house the employees of Short Bros., the aircraft manufacturers, felt particularly strongly the loss of its wartime prosperity, and when Sir Samuel Hoare announced in early November 1924 that he would inspect the works at Cardington it was believed that he might make a pronouncement of importance to the future of the whole district, for the Conservative Government, in which he was Air Minister, had inherited the airship scheme from the Socialists and were determined to follow it up.

'It is a matter of great satisfaction that we are attempting seriously to develop airships,' said Sir Samuel. 'The importance of the development that we are undertaking cannot be overemphasized. There have been disasters to airships in the past, and we mean to make the fullest use of the experience gained from those unfortunate events. We mean to do everything humanly possible to eliminate danger in connection with airships.'

This news naturally delighted all who heard it, and a writer in the *Bedfordshire Record* confidently declared that 'Bedford cannot avoid a boom'. Previous attempts to make the Government conscious of local hardships had failed, for other parts of the country were in an even worse state. Mr S R Wells, the MP for Bedford Division, had repeatedly tried to persuade them to reopen the aerodrome during the previous three years to help the unemployment problem, and it was recalled that Commander Sir Dennistoun Burney - whose company would build the R.100 - had predicted at a dinner of the Bedford Chamber of Trade two years earlier that Cardington might become the English centre of an Imperial airship service between England and India.

One shed at Cardington had been kept fairly busy since the war with a programme of refitting the R.33, and this was a magnet for Sir Samuel Hoare and his party. The airships were so large that they fitted their sheds with only a foot or two to spare on either side, and R.33 was no exception. As a mild joke the staff liked to lead visitors who were new to airships through a door in the middle of the shed, so that they came immediately face to face with what seemed to be a gigantic silver wall stretching from floor to ceiling. Then they would petulantly ask their guide: 'But where *is* the airship?' and the guide would reply, 'That's it - ahead of you! All of it!'

For the airship was so vast that it filled the entire shed, hanging like some gigantic silver fish in a closely-tailored cave, neither floating freely nor yet resting on the ground, but secured by ropes in a sickly sweet atmosphere of dope with which the canvas was treated. Even on that day when all seemed bright, a reminder of an earlier airship failure was close at hand: the R.37, which workmen were dismantling, but she was wisely kept in the background, on the south side of the shed, away from the visitors and indeed shielded from their gaze. Despite an expenditure of £325,000 she had never been finished, and indeed never left her shed.

This sad sight was not to be remarked on at such a time of promise, however, for the new airships would be larger, faster and safer than any that had gone before; the R. 101 would be 720 feet long, almost twice as long as St Paul's Cathedral was high. As originally visualized, she would have five engines to fly her across the face of the earth, and much was made of the weight of passengers and freight that she would be able to carry, although it was pointed out that on a flight to a hot country, this might have to be cut to about a third, for technical reasons, which would mean that barely 20 tons were available for freight or paying passengers. This caused no lessening of the general satisfaction, however, and, looking back, it seems surprising that pride over this performance should have been so great, for here was a vessel as large as the largest ocean liner, and yet on an Eastern journey barely capable of carrying a load that could be drawn by a lorry and a trailer. This incongruity of performance was further emphasized by the fact that besides linking the outer marches of the Empire in a speedy way, the immediate aim of this enterprise was to demonstrate that airships could be used, like ships at sea, for commercial purposes and on a paying basis.

'There are difficulties in achieving success in devising these vehicles of travel, which appear to be almost inherent in their nature,' wrote Viscount Simon. 'Water is about 800 times heavier than air and it follows that if you want to build a large vessel which is going to float in the air, you must make it 800 times lighter than a vessel which is going to float, like a submarine in the sea. To devise an airship which is about as big as the *Mauretania,* in the hope of being able to carry 60 tons over and above its fixed weight, seems to give little promise of profitable use.'[3]

This view was not shared publicly - at least by any who heard of the proposed plans at Cardington that day - and plans went ahead at a great pace. Mooring masts would be established not only at Ismailia, near the Suez Canal, and at Karachi, in India, to accommodate airships between their flights but also at St Hubert, near Montreal, in Canada and a fourth was planned for Australia. Full facilities for carrying out overhauls at these Empire termini and staging posts were being arranged; the airship engines, for instance, were to be so ingeniously designed that they could be changed while the ships were actually moored in the air.

Although the idea of linking the Empire countries was undoubtedly sound, the planning of this regular airship service was being worked out in terms of the sea and of ships, because there was no other comparable basis. Flying was still novel, without long traditions of its own, and airships, in any case, had for many years been closely associated with the Navy. There was, however, far more in planning an airship programme than just building an airship, and as a result of agreements made at the Dominions Conference of 1926, land for sites was surveyed in many Empire countries, and, at the request of their Governments, a party of experts from the British Airship and Meteorological Departments examined possible sites in Ceylon, in St Helena, Africa and elsewhere with a view to the future. St Hubert, Montreal, which had been selected as the Canadian base, was designed to receive airships and aeroplanes. It is now used by the Royal Canadian Air Force.

A site was also surveyed in South Africa, roughly forty miles north of Durban, at Groutville, and the Australian Government agreed to buy one near Perth. They prudently decided that nothing further would be done until the two airships, R. 100 and R.101, had successfully completed their trials; and New Zealand, too, cast about for a suitable site, but making the same conditions.

At this point, all hung on the flying trials, for nothing much further could be said or done until the airships themselves had shown what they could do. Experts had provisionally worked out how their timetable would compare with sailing times, basing their calculations in part on the recent passenger and freight achievements of the *Graf Zeppelin,* which was shuttling between Germany and South America. Erring on the side of caution they allowed an average flying speed for the R.101 of only 50 miles an hour, rather less than the German ship had achieved. They were careful to point out that maintaining even such a low average speed depended on the airship's own reliability and lightness, and they insisted that only actual flying trials could show whether these problems had been successfully solved by the prototype R. 101.

Keeping to a timetable in the air meant that full allowance had to be made for the weather, and for the first time meteorological conditions over the whole route were recorded in chart form, and the distribution of wind and weather over Europe, the Mediterranean and India were analysed in daily detail. Other charts showed the direction of upper wind along the airship's route. Thunderstorms and their frequency were also investigated, and so were wind and temperature conditions at the different bases, for all had a vital bearing on the safety of the ship.

Four anemometers were installed at Cardington to record such hazards as wind eddies and their rate of travel. At Ismailia and

Karachi, where temperature was the essential factor, engineers built a 200-foot mast, equipped at different levels with electrically recording thermometers, and during the hot season the data thus obtained was examined for the benefit of the airship staff before they began their first flight.

It was the most thorough experiment ever made into weather forecasting, for the great airship was almost entirely at the mercy of the elements, and could be driven miles off her course by heavy wind. When the *Graf Zeppelin* flew to America for the first time, her Captain took her no less than 1,000 miles off course to avoid a storm of exceptional velocity. For the benefit of the R.101 flights, meteorological centres across Europe and Asia were to pool their information; stations at Malta, Ismailia, Baghdad, Karachi, and Aden forwarded the results of their observations. At Cardington a new meteorological building was constructed and the forecast room, on an upper floor, was equipped with wireless receivers as well as recording instruments. The whole block was so built that the duty officer at his weather charts would at the same time have an uninterrupted view of the sky all round, while his instruments were continuously recording weather observations all the time. An anemometer mast, as high as the mooring mast, ensured that the wind at its height could also be recorded. Continuous day and night watch was kept by scientists with a trained technical staff; and from this room weather messages could be transmitted to the airship, which would also be in radio contact with other centres along the route.

Both R. 100 and R. 101 were equipped with long-wave sets for transmitting and receiving signals over a range up to 2,000 miles. They also carried auxiliary sets that could send and receive messages up to 400 miles, and a radio telephone range up to 100 miles. It was further proposed to experiment with direction-finding apparatus and short-wave transmitters, and the Air Ministry even talked of installing a 'wireless picture receiver' so that they could receive weather maps from the meteorological forecasting stations on their route. It was ironic that, after these years of preparations to ensure that the world's weather could be revealed at the touch of a switch, no foreknowledge of storms could save the airship from beginning her trial journey. And the longest message sent out during that voyage over R.101's magnificent radio was the intelligence that 'after an excellent supper our distinguished passengers smoked a final cigar and have gone to bed to rest after the excitement of their leave-taking'.

The design and eventual construction work involved was tremendous, a fact that the public, conditioned to expect quick and startling benefits from this new flying ship, completely ignored, and indeed were encouraged to ignore, for one announcement promised that R.101 would be ready for preliminary trials within two years, and would make her first trip to India well within three, that is, by the early spring of 1927.

This early completion date was hailed as a magnificent achievement. It was much more than that; it was impossible, as Colonel Vincent Richmond, the chief designer of R. 101, hinted when he addressed a luncheon of the Bedford Rotary Club in March, 1926, on the subject of airships and their future. Someone asked him when his own airship would be ready, and he replied cautiously that she was due to be finished at the end of next year, but he asked for sympathetic consideration of that estimate, 'owing to the experimental nature of the work'.

This was the first admission that delays were likely, and by April 1927, three years after the decision to construct two airships - and when R. 101 should have been preparing for her maiden voyage to India - little had been done about even laying her down. Work on R. 100 was already at an advanced stage at Howden, but the Air Minister announced that it was still not expected to lay R. 101 down 'for another two months or more'.

Lord Thomson, the Socialist Air Minister, who was in office at the start and completion of the Airship Programme, had budgeted for a total expenditure of £1,350,000 on these two airships over three years, but it was later admitted that 'both the period and the cost were under-estimated'. Estimates of expenditure at Cardington for these years alone totalled £770,000, which was more than twice the estimated cost of R. 100, and it was by no means clear where this money had gone, for supporters of the State scheme seemed able to produce little to show for such a vast expenditure.

At least £13,000 of it had been spent on reconditioning R.36, which had been completed in April, 1921, suffered a serious accident in June, and never flew again. She had been laid up until someone suggested flying her to Egypt on an experimental journey to gather data for future voyages by R.101. But by the time she was reconditioned and brought up to standard for such a long flight, the whole idea of making it had been abandoned. Altogether, this airship only flew for a total of 97 hours.

Then, in January, 1926, the Auditor-General admitted that the Air Ministry had placed a contract for girder work with a private firm, which should have been completed by the end of the year, but since the Design Staff at Cardington kept changing their designs, delays occurred in fowarding details of these structural alterations to the contractors involved. As a result, the contract was broken, and the Air Ministry was faced with paying out £14,800 to the firm as compensation. The Auditor-General also had to report a further unsatisfactory transaction resulting in considerable financial loss to the State. The Air Ministry, it appeared, had purchased some tons of ferro-silicon for use in building their airship and then, apparently under the impression that they had bought too much, had sold what was believed to be surplus for £4 a ton. It was then discovered that they had, in fact, bought not too much but far too little, and so they were faced with the prospect of buying back what they had sold - but at £20 a ton.

Then a complete section of the airship was built at Cardington at a cost of £40,000, with the idea of calculating various strains and stresses which the complete airship would have to undergo. At Howden, the design staff of the R. 100, who could not afford to spend money like this, for their airship was being built by a private enterprise concern on an economic basis, relied on paper calculations before they began to build. Seemingly their way had better results, for R.100 successfully flew to Canada and back, and altogether covered more than 20,000 miles with only normal wear and tear.

Yet, despite this prodigious expense and wastage, there were certain, often foolish, attempts to economize. The Cardington team, for instance, needed a calculating machine, which would cost about £50, so that the engineers working on the mathematical stressing of the airship could save themselves much needless work and also produce quicker results. What a mathematician would take twenty hours - two and a half working days - to calculate, this machine could do in under an hour. Although the saving in time and money would obviously be immense, the request was firmly refused.

Both Sir Samuel Hoare and Lord Thomson, as successive Air Ministers, were under almost constant attack by critics, such as Mr

Rose, who knew nothing professionally of the problems involved and seemed to care less. These criticisms received full publicity and this in time caused pressure to be put on the men working at Cardington, for the only satisfactory way to silence criticism was to show the airship flying successfully.

In the meantime, critics were answered by hasty and ill-conceived explanations, such as the news that the R. 101 could be used for naval reconnaissance work. Possibly she could - if no enemy aircraft were near to shoot her down - but no one in authority added that the Admiralty had been given no say whatsoever in her construction, nor indeed had their Lordships' views been invited. In the House of Commons, the cost was also criticized severely, for a great deal of money seemed to have been spent without any real grasp of the duty and function of the finished airship. The Air Minister of the time - either Lord Thomson or Sir Samuel Hoare - replied patiently that the R. 101 would 'satisfactorily meet the demands and requirements of all three services'. She could be used to transport troops, for naval reconnaissance work, and even - as R.33 had been used - as an aerial carrier for smaller aircraft. These claims aroused the annoyance of a writer in the *Evening Standard,* who declared: 'Considering she is also intended to be a commercial vessel for the conveyance of passengers and mails between Britain and India, the versatility that is to be demanded of her borders on the magical.' For the Air Ministry to be building an airship which, for all that might be said about service duties, was intended primarily for civilian use, seemed to many as anachronistic as for the Admiralty to busy themselves with the construction of an ocean liner for paying passengers.

Despite these criticisms about the cost of the R.101, there is no doubt that her size and even her expense added much to the legend of her invincibility. Since she was bigger and more expensive than anything that had ever been built to fly and embodied far more new ideas, it seemed to follow as a natural consequence that she would be the best and the safest.

In mid-November, 1926, at the Imperial Conference in London, the Prime Ministers of the Dominions most likely to be affected by the airship service inspected a scale model of R.101, and pronounced themselves greatly impressed. At least one observer with the party was astounded at the air of opulence. The R. 101/ he wrote afterwards, 'will provide luxuries undreamed of by Jules Verne and H G Wells. It will positively be an aerial hotel.'

It was all that; but more emphasis had been placed on ingenuity of construction and design, on comfort and the high standard of all the fittings, than on the purpose for which the vessel was basically intended: to fly safely in all weathers. When Sir Samuel Hoare took the Dominion Prime Ministers to Cardington on this occasion to show them the model and the site of this great endeavour, and also the airship R.33 in flight -this difficulty was almost embarrassingly apparent, for R.33 was so vulnerable and hard to handle in anything like strong weather that what Sir Samuel later described as 'a very gentle wind' made it impossible to pull her out of her shed. This did not augur well for a regular airship service operating in all weathers and to a time schedule.

Although the design team was generally considered the best available - and, indeed, most of the British experts of all branches of airship construction were involved - the importance of saving weight was not recognized until the last few months. All decisions governing the thickness of girders allowed a great safety margin. If there was any discussion about two thicknesses of metal that could be used in the airship, the thicker and heavier was always chosen. The engines also were very heavy, for it was decided to power her with five diesel engines, for which two main advantages were claimed. First, they would be cheaper to run than the conventional petrol engines, for fuel oil then cost only £5 a ton, as against £23 for petrol, and this would naturally mean a great saving when the airship was used for commercial purposes over long distances. The second factor influencing the designers was that fuel oil was, generally speaking, non-inflammable, and this was a great asset on a journey to India or to any other hot country, and a great comfort to those who were concerned at the thought of their proximity to five and a half million cubic feet of dangerously inflammable hydrogen. This oil would burn under pressure or at a very high temperature, but not if it came into casual contact with a flame or spark in the open air. Wing Commander T R Cave-Browne-Cave, who had charge of the airship engine department at Cardington, and who did an enormous amount of experimental work with the engines, demonstrated this virtue to a party of distinguished visitors by picking up a blowlamp and applying the flame to an open tin of diesel oil. Nothing happened. He then directed the flame on to a small open can of petrol, which immediately flared up, to his visitors' alarm. He reassured them, however, and then emptied the diesel oil over the flames. The fire went out at once. Diesel engines, however, had never before been used to power any British airship or aeroplane, and so none were immediately available, and a compromise had to be reached whereby two four-cylinder diesel engines, which had been primarily intended for powering Canadian locomotives, were redesigned to make one eight-cylinder engine. The designers had hoped that each of these five beautifully made Beardmore Mark I Tornado engines would be able to maintain 700 brake horsepower at a thousand revolutions a minute. Tests showed, however, that they were slower and less powerful than had been intended, and could only develop and maintain 585 horsepower, with a possible maximum of 650 for very short periods. And since they had originally been destined for railway use, where weight was an asset because it gave traction to the engine wheels, they were naturally very strong and heavy, as of course any compression ignition engine made to withstand great internal pressure must be. Although modifications were made to lighten them, it was found with some gloom that the five engines weighed a total of seventeen tons, compared with nine tons for the conventional Rolls-Royce Condor aero engines, which Commander Burney was fitting to the R.100, and against only seven tons for the *Graf Zeppelin's* engines. In favour of the diesel engines it was argued that they would only need seventeen tons of fuel oil to carry the airship a distance of 2,500 miles, as opposed to twenty-three tons of petrol which would propel R. 100 for a similar distance.

The engines of any new aircraft sometimes have prolonged teething troubles. These were no exception. The principle of the diesel engine is that a small quantity of fuel oil is injected into each cylinder, and then under great pressure as the piston goes up the cylinder it ignites spontaneously and drives the piston down. Their speed is controlled by regulating the amount of oil that is injected, but a system satisfactory under all flying conditions had not been perfected by the time they were installed. This meant that the engines were not very sensitive to fine adjustments of speed, with a consequent effect on the handling and placing of the airship.

Although R. 101 was fitted with a rudder to bring her round, her commander would place an almost equal reliance on control by his engines, as a ship's captain of a twin-screw vessel can steer on the propellers. The only means of slowing or reversing an airship in the sky was, of course, by reversing the engines, for owing to her streamlined shape there was little resistance to the air. Consequently if her engines were shut off she would just continue to drift on her own momentum until a chance crosswind changed her direction. The idea of throwing out a rear parachute as an air brake, which is now used to slow down some jet aeroplanes on landing, had not then been put into practice.

The airship commander, on approaching the mooring mast, had to be certain he had enough "backward thrust' first to slow and finally to halt his vessel, otherwise he would either overshoot the mast or worse still, go right into it, as had happened previously when wind blew the R.33 into her masthead. The designers thus decided to fit propellers of an intricate and ingenious design with blades that could be feathered and completely reversed, so that they could drive the airship backwards as well as forwards without having to reverse the engines. This idea received support from Mr Harry Leech, the foreman at the Royal Airship Works, because he had seen such propellers of variable pitch successfully fitted to an Italian airship as long ago as 1918.

Harry Leech had spent several years in the Royal Naval Air Service during the war on patrol in balloons, over the North Sea, and in late 1918 he was sent from Pulham to collect an airship from Italy. He travelled by train from Le Havre to Rome (there seemed nothing incongruous at that stage of the war in being able to cross the continent so easily) and then flew the airship back; it was a semi-rigid ship and was fitted with hollow steel propeller blades that could be feathered. When Leech was testing the engines for R.101, he realized how valuable such feathering qualities would be for that airship, which had airscrews 18 feet 6 inches long, and he did a great deal of experimental work with them. They would rig up one of the big Beardmore engines at the far end of the hangar, complete with propeller, and then all round these dangerous blades they hung screens made from two sets of wartime steel torpedo netting, which had been suspended vertically in harbour entrances to stop the entry of submarines or torpedoes.

'It was as well we did so,' he said later. "The metal blades just would not stand up to the strain, and neither did the hubs. The blades suffered metal fatigue at the roots, and before we knew where we were the engine had flung them out on the net, and was racing away on its own.'

It would probably have been possible to fit variable pitch propellers had further time been available for more experiments, but this was only one of the new ideas the R. 101 was to incorporate, and there just was not time to try them all thoroughly and to bring them up to a standard of perfection. So much time and Government money had already been spent, and Press and Parliament were growing increasingly impatient for results.

'Year after year.. .for the whole length of the Parliament, I had to meet a full-scale attack whenever I introduced the Air Estimates,' wrote Sir Samuel Hoare. ' "When are you going to bring your two old horses out of the stall?" "What have you to show for the hundreds of thousands of pounds that you are spending every year on them?" My only answer was to play all the possible variations on Asquith's "Wait and See" and to report that the experiment was a very new one and must be given time...'4

Time: the estimated date for the launching came and went, and still the engines were not working satisfactorily. Since they could not have variable pitch propellers, there was no point in having metal blades at all, and so they reverted to the cheaper and lighter wooden propellers, that had a fixed boss. These propellers were simply fixed with strong steel bolts to the end of the crankshaft of the engine, and it was hoped that they would give no more trouble. This hope was not realized.

The propeller blades were based on a very strong centre, but even this was still not stout enough to cope with the enormous, surging thrust of the big eight-cylinder engines. As soon as the engines accelerated, the bosses of the wooden propellers cracked under the strain, and within a short time the engine was racing away, having torn out the whole centre of the propeller, as a knife cuts out the core of an apple. The propeller would thus either spin slowly or fall right off the end of the crankshaft. In either case it was quite useless, and highly dangerous.

Mr Leech recalls the first time this type of trouble occurred at the Beardmore factory, when they rigged an engine on a gantry and started it. One blade snapped off almost immediately.

'The engine went into a dance and tore itself up,' he said. 'We found the blade embedded in the ground three-quarters of a mile away.'

This expensive and dangerous habit of 'chuggling' or tearing out the heart of the propeller, was finally cured by clamping sheets of emery cloth between the boss of each propeller and the hub nave plate, and then each propeller was secured by twelve bolts of high-tensile steel.

The easiest way to reverse the airship now seemed to be by carrying the fifth engine simply as a 'passenger' while they were flying forward, and only to use it when they stopped the other four, and wished to reverse. This was not an ideal solution for it meant that for all forward flights of the airship an engine which, with its car, weighed rather more than three tons, would be carried as useless weight, simply to have it available for a few minutes at the end of each journey while they slowed down enough to approach their mooring mast, and to back away from the mast again when they set off. Added to this dead weight, the cruising speed of the airship would also suffer, for instead of having five engines to drive her along, she would have only four, and since none of the engines was as powerful as had been expected, her speeds would be lamentably low. No one really liked this decision, and eventually it was changed a second time, so that when the airship finally set off for Egypt, all five engines were working ahead, but the two forward engines were provided with means whereby the engineers could stop them, alter the valve timing and start them again, so that they were running the wrong way round.

Having solved this problem, the engineers next tackled the equally serious problem of weight. The engines had steel crankcases that were hopelessly heavy for airship use, and so new ones were cast in aluminium, which solved the problem of weight but presented a problem of another kind: the resonance of the engine cracked them.

Since the engines had been intended for much harder work than spinning a wooden propeller, the big-ends began to give trouble, but this was cured by having the bearings gold-plated. Finally, when the engines were really running well, it was found that they had two periods of destructive frequency; at between 350 and 400 revolutions a minute, which was the suggested idling speed, and again at 820 rpm, when they would be driving the airship at her cruising speed, the engines began to vibrate and tremble in an alarming manner. To avoid these periods they had to be run rather faster than was desirable when they were idling, and instead of cruising at around 800 revolutions a minute the engines had to be accelerated up to 950 rpm, which was uncomfortably close to their maximum. A good deal of trouble with fractured fuel pipes and oil tank fittings was experienced until this solution was reached.

At Howden the Airship Guarantee Company, working on the R. 100, were also having engine trouble, for their first intention had been to use a specially-designed engine which would run on a mixture of hydrogen and paraffin - and a similar project had been mooted at Cardington. Nothing came of the hydrocarbon engine at either place, however, and after a year's work the R. 100 team abandoned the idea and concentrated on diesel engines of the same size and type that were being installed in the State airship. After six months or so it was decided that these were also unsuitable, for they were still virtually in the experimental stage, and too heavy for use in aircraft; they weighed eight pounds for each horsepower they developed against roughly half this weight per horsepower of a comparable petrol engine, and much work remained to be done on them. Instead of searching for a new way of powering the R.100, Sir Dennistoun Burney's team went back to the tried Rolls-Royce aero engines, which worked well on every flight the airship made - although they were actually secondhand!

The difference between the two enterprises is tragically illustrated by these approaches to the same fundamental problem. The private business concern realized when they were following a wrong course and abandoned it, selling off their equipment for the best price they could get. The State concern, however, heavy with the burden of public money for which they would have to account before Parliament, could not afford to abandon what they had already begun, however unsuitable the early experiments might be. The reputation, the future, even possibly the jobs of the men concerned - and so many families were involved in that time of national depression - could hinge on the success or failure of their task. They could not go back, but were forced to keep on, trying desperately to equate haste with safety, for as fast as one problem was solved, another arose.

The R.101 engines, for example, were 'pushers', with the propellers behind them, and so that they would not throw too great a strain on the supports holding each car, a heavy steel rope ran back from the centre of each propeller hub to the side of the airship. This had the effect of taking up part of the jerky thrust of the engine and spreading it, but more research into the construction of supports for the engines might have done away with such a crude and clumsy method. Again this would have required time: and time was the one thing that no one connected with the construction of R. 101 could afford to spare.

Then, since the diesel engines were started by small petrol starting engines it was pointed out that petrol was being carried in any case, and would present as much danger of fire in a tropical climate as if the main engines were also petrol-driven. Thus, in the last stages of design, plans were made to replace the petrol engines with small oil engines; and, in fact, one had already been replaced when the R. 101 set off on her voyage.

There was no time to alter the others, however, no time to think again, for by then time was the enemy of everyone connected with the airship. There was nothing to do but go on and hope for the best.

1. *Slide Rule* (House of Stratus, 2000).
2. *Empire of the Air* (Collins).
3. Viscount Simon, *Retrospect* (Hutchinson, 1952).
4.   Viscount Templewood, *Empire of the Air* (Collins).

CHAPTER FOUR
Work Done

In 1924, when work first started on R.101, time was not so pressing. Indeed, there seemed enough time to test, to try and possibly to discard all novel ideas that were submitted for use in this ambitious attempt to build the world's biggest and most modern airship. No one had any doubt that the airship would be all this and more; everyone associated with her - first, the designers and the draughtsmen, and then the fitters and riggers who swarmed about the gigantic skeleton in the cold and draughty shed at Cardington - were sure of this.

Although it was sometimes said in the R.100's hangar when the two airships were almost complete and ready for their trials: 'No ship built at Cardington *ever* flies for long,' such defeatist talk was never heard from those most intimately connected with her building. No airship ever built in Britain had such care and hard work put into her: and no airship ever built in Britain had been the subject of such careful calculations extending over six years. So much depended on her, and therefore on those who built her, that they felt themselves an honoured band, and they were willing to work long and difficult hours on their 'ship' to make her the best in the world.

"There, beneath the huge shed, at that time the largest building in the world,' wrote Sir Samuel Hoare, 'under the shadow of the towering landing mast, and face to face with the monster of silk and steel, they lived and worked like a religious community intent upon their single purpose..."

Colonel Vincent Richmond, the Chief Designer, who had travelled in Germany and studied the Zeppelins, and who for years before he had begun work on R.101 had carried in his mind the germ of such an airship, used to say to his wife: 'I am one of the most fortunate of men, for I earn my livelihood doing what I love most in the world.'

At that time they had a house in Goldington Road, Bedford, called The Cottage, although it was, in fact, large and roomy, and here Vincent Richmond had his study on the ground floor looking out on to the side garden. On one wall was a huge wooden four-bladed propeller from one of the early airships, the leading edge of the blades beautifully bound with leather. He worked there all day at first, and then, when his office at Cardington was ready, he brought home urgent work in the evenings.

Many people would visit them in Bedford - Air Ministry officials, aeronautical enthusiasts, passing Air Force officers with airship experience - for Richmond was both very popular and an entertaining host. Later, as work went on, Boulton & Paul, the engineering firm who made the girders, presented him with a set of stereoscopic photographs, with viewing glasses through which visitors could see for themselves the astonishing and almost terrifying size of the aerial ship, and this became an added attraction for the visitors. The Richmonds both liked the country and eventually decided to move a few miles out from Bedford, and there, surrounded by miles and miles of flat fields - the best 'airship country' in the world - Vincent Richmond could work his very long hours without fear of being disturbed.

'Often he used to work through the night until the birds were twittering,' Mrs Richmond says, and yet he was not a man to be dulled by work or borne down by the weight of worries. He played a hard game of tennis which was the more remarkable because as a boy he had been seriously ill, and for a time could move around only in a wheelchair. Always a man to turn stumbling blocks into stepping stones, this enforced inactivity made him determined to put his time to the best use, and he began to study engineering, with special attention to aeronautical problems.

On Sundays, he often used to read the lesson at Odell church, or sometimes drove over to Highams Park, where he had lived before his marriage, to preach a sermon, for he was a qualified lay reader. His talks were always plain and to the point: even in his religion he thought like an engineer and presented his arguments lucidly. Both he and his wife were also very fond of music, but neither this nor anything else came between him and R.101. Sometimes they would drive back from a concert in London, and despite the late hour, the urge to work would grip him, and he would pull off his dinner jacket, put on a dressing-gown and start again. His wife, meanwhile, used to sit by the study fire, knitting or reading, and each would be glad of the other's presence, saying nothing. And then, at some time in the early morning Richmond would push back his chair, stand up, stretch his arms above his head and say: 'Well, I'm going to do no more tonight.'

Although, like the wives of all those engaged on building this behemoth, Florence Richmond knew little about the technical problems of airships, nothing else was as important. The airship dominated them all. The other wives lived closer to Cardington, many of them in Shortstown, and they could tell when to expect their husbands home for tea by the roar of returning engines. They were accustomed to long and unexpected separations when things went wrong in some experiment; they endured meals on their own, made sandwiches for their husbands and never lost patience when engagements they had looked forward to for weeks were suddenly cancelled. There was never any need to ask the reason. It was always the same: the airship.

Some wives had been doing this ever since their marriage. One was Mrs Mary Gent, wife of William Gent, the Chief Engineer in R.101, who had been interested in flying since the stick-and-string days of aeronautical pioneering before the First World War. As a young bride her first home was at Erith, in Kent, on the Thames, where her husband was working with Sir Hiram Maxim on the first British aero engine, long since deposited in the South Kensington Science Museum. The early trials of this engine had also been quite a trial to Mary Gent, but she helped as the wives usually did, in unspectacular but very necessary ways. Every night she would, for instance, set her alarm clock for three o'clock next morning, and then go out on the little balcony of her house in Pier Road, near the river, and hold up a pocket handkerchief to test the strength of the wind. If the handkerchief fluttered, there was wind about, and she could go back to bed without waking her husband, for the aeroplanes on test were so frail that the slightest wind added danger to the experiments. The best chance of a windless flight lay in the early hours before sunrise, and so if her handkerchief hung limply in her hand, she had to awaken her husband, so that he could collect a car and drive over to Joyce Green, outside Dartford, for the trials.

In July, 1919, William Gent had flown in the British airship R.34 to America and back, the first double crossing of the Atlantic by an airship, so, like all other airship wives, she was used to his being away from home for long periods and thinking, talking, living airships to the exclusion of almost everything else. She spent much time with her son, Lawrence, while her husband was in Scotland at the factory that made his precious engines. Airships to him and to his colleagues were not just a way of earning a living, a job to be done in set hours; they were a vocation, for the enthusiasm of the pioneers was infectious. Nothing was to be rushed or done without trial in those early days, when they had time to spare. As Professor (now Sir) Richard Southwell, who presided over the Airship Stressing Panel, put it: 'We are proceeding with healthy cold feet', an apt description, for with a design bristling with new ideas, caution was necessary.

First of all, and most important, instead of building the R. 101 empirically and by rule of thumb (techniques which had, unfortunately, characterized too many previous attempts to build British airships) two models were tested thoroughly at the National Physical Laboratory over a period of two years, from 1924 to 1926. The model that seemed most promising was then selected for further work and designs based on this shape were begun. It was fatter in proportion to its length than previous airships, and looked much thicker in flight than the German Zeppelins. In fact, the shape of R.101 was such a nearly perfect streamline that it offered negligible resistance to the air.

The news that R.101 would have steel girders came as a surprise to many airship experts, for duralumin or wood had been the chief materials used in previous airships. Duralumin was the speciality of the Zeppelins; and laminated three-ply wood had been used extensively by the German Schutte-Lanz concern, and in some smaller British airships that had been copied from them without notable success.

These 'wooden' airships showed alarming tendencies in flight, and a pilot who was to deliver one to the airship station at East Fortune in Scotland, landed at Howden in Yorkshire instead, and refused to go any further. 'The gangway should have been straight,' the Coxswain explained, 'but as soon as we got in the air it began to twist and turn like a worm. It was like flying in a wriggling eel.' A repair team at once went aboard to see whether they could strengthen the airship for the second lap of the journey, and one man fell down between two gasbags, but landed safely and unhurt on a stay at the bottom of the envelope. Here he lay trapped in this huge silver cavern until ladders could be run up from the ground and a hole cut through the fabric to release him.

One of the few traditional features to be incorporated in the design of R. 101 was the use of goldbeater's skin to make the gasbags. Looking back from a world of nylon, polythene and miracles in plastic, the use of these skins seems incredibly anachronistic. They were, in fact, membranes that had formed part of a bullock's intestine known as the caecum, and the method of their preparation and use was crude, messy and almost mediaeval.

First, lengths of this skin, measuring about 35 by 30 inches, were cleansed of all fat in tubs of warm water, and then teams of girls scraped them carefully with blunt knives. They were then stored in tubs of brine until they were needed, when the girls soaked them in glycerine and stretched them onto a great sheet of canvas, still dripping wet, so that their edges would stick together. When dry they were peeled off the canvas like an enormous roll of parchment, and afterwards they were varnished. These skins had all been specially imported from meat-canning firms in Chicago, and it was estimated that more than a million oxen contributed to enable the R. 101 to take the air. The gasbags were all far larger than any ever fitted previously in an airship; the largest contained 510,300 cubic feet of hydrogen, and was so big that it could not have been completely inflated inside Westminster Hall.

One of the main difficulties that had faced all previous designers of airships was to find a satisfactory means of releasing gas from the gasbags as the airship rose in the sky. When the air pressure decreased, so the gas within the bag expanded - as the Due de Chartres had found in 1796 when his flying fish of an airship made her maiden voyage, and he had to pierce the envelope with a flagstaff to let the gas out before the whole thing burst. Such a balloon without a rigid frame could be controlled by throwing ballast over the side to make it lighter and so gain height, and brought down to earth again by gradually 'valving' (releasing) gas until it began to fall. Rigid airships built before R. 101 had been equipped with valves of a very simple design, loaded with a spring which opened when the airship rose above what was called her 'pressure height' - the height at which the gas completely filled all bags - and to allow for this expansion, the gasbags could never be completely inflated while the airship was at her mooring mast. Since the gas used was lighter than air, the valves in previous airships had been fixed underneath the bags, because if they had been on top, all the gas within the bag would have escaped as soon as they were opened. Thus, whenever a tear or a rent occurred in the fabric of a gasbag, only the gas below the rent would escape; the nearer the rent to the top of the bag, the more serious it became. These orthodox spring-loaded valves operated automatically when the gas reached a certain pressure. Other valves were also fitted for manoeuvring purposes and these could be opened or closed from the control car. Gas valves of both these proved types were used with success in the private enterprise airship, R. 100.

The gas valves devised for the R.101, however, like so much else, were of a new and ingenious design, patented by Colonel Richmond and Squadron-Leader Rope, and instead of being fitted on top of each gasbag, they were fixed halfway up on two sides. For the larger bags, valves measuring three feet four inches in diameter were used; the smaller valves were two feet six across. They were all of extremely sensitive design and it was estimated that an increase of pressure, amounting to only two millimetres of water, was sufficient to open the valve completely. The position of the valves meant that should the airship be flying at an altitude close to her pressure height and suddenly roll unexpectedly, a lot of gas would be lost when, in fact, the commander would not wish to lose any. The valves were almost too delicate in their operation, tests showing that the airship would only have to roll through five degrees for them to start opening. Even at her mooring mast she frequently rolled more than this.

A further disadvantage about the new type of valve was its inaccessibility. With the old type, which rested on stands near a ropewalk easily reached by riggers, a sticking valve could be adjusted very quickly, and since it was underneath the gasbag, very little gas would escape. The new type, however, being fitted halfway up the bag, and probably 100 feet up inside the airship, were much more difficult to reach and, should one jam open, far more gas would escape before it could be repaired.

There was a further point against the loss of gas, although a relatively minor one, and this was economy. While hydrogen was nowhere nearly as expensive as helium, it was by no means cheap, and to fill the largest gasbag cost between £700 and £800. Thus any leaks were worrying on the score of expense as well as of safety. The valves on R.101 really did two jobs, for they allowed excess gas to escape and were also used by the Commander when he wished to manoeuvre the airship either through heavy weather or to bring her down when approaching the mooring mast. Although the airship had elevators which, within limits, would help her up into the sky or bring her down, the most satisfactory way of manoeuvring her on landing was to release some gas and let her own weight bring her down.

The gasbags themselves were contained within enormous harnesses of wire, rather like the harness that hangs from a parachute, a system of suspension that had again been devised and patented by Colonel Richmond and Squadron-Leader Rope. This wiring strengthened the gasbags against a sudden unexpected increase in internal pressure, and also communicated the lifting power of the gas in the bags to the airship. There was a third essential for the wiring harnesses; they had to hold the very delicate bags away from any sharp projections within the airship which could easily pierce them. Indeed, one of the advantages which Richmond and Rope had claimed for their invention, and which was actually mentioned in the Patent Specification, was that it kept the gasbags 'from touching the longitudinal girders'. Later, as the airship became heavier and heavier, loaded down with so much equipment and the weight of so many new and brilliant ideas, the gasbag wiring was let out as far as possible so that more gas could be pumped in, for there was a danger that all this ingenuity, all this expense, and all this work, would produce an airship of unparalleled size and complication which might perhaps fly, but not with the load for which she had been originally intended. When the wiring was loosed to this unexpected extent it was found that the gasbags did in fact touch some of the girders under certain conditions, and out of this arose further troubles.

The harness involved literally hundreds of wires that surrounded and braced and were connected to the seventeen gasbags, and these wires were all brought down in such a way that should one gasbag become either partially or completely deflated in flight, then the new conditions of pressure would be distributed equally along the entire frame of the airship. The whole arrangement was very clever and highly regarded by the knowledgeable; indeed Major F A de V Robertson, writing in *Flight* (30 August, 1928), declared that it was 'one of the most brilliant and progressive features of the design of R.101'.

The size of almost every part of the airship was so vast that it was decided to make the component members elsewhere. This again was a novel suggestion, for the Zeppelins had been largely built in place at Friedrichshafen; the R.101, however, was built in sections at the works of Boulton & Paul in Norwich, and then assembled in her shed at

Cardington. This method of working is now very common, especially in the motor industry, where components from half-a-dozen proprietary firms are assembled under one roof, and the resulting vehicle is called by the name of the assembling factory. So exact were the calculations, and so brilliantly had Boulton & Paul's engineers carried out the instructions of the designers, that machining was done with tolerances ranging from .015 of an inch in a girder 11 feet long to .03 of an inch in one of 30 feet. When the time came to assemble these girders, that resembled parts from a giant Meccano set, the engineers laid a line down the centre of the shed, using a theodolite and other measuring instruments, and then work started amidships and moved both fore and aft at the same time. To visitors, the shed looked like the Crystal Palace, and presented an astonishing spectacle of activity. Gigantic metal girders criss-crossed into the vast dimness of the roof as the great airship took shape. Workmen in rubber-soled shoes climbed hand over foot with drills and hammers, apparently oblivious of the height and the draughts in the great building. Ropes hung down from the ceiling, and many used these instead of the firemen's ladders. At one end of the shed a visitor saw a gigantic wheel 400 feet round, like something which had escaped from a fairground. This was one of the sections which were constructed on the ground and then were raised to the roof by tackle and lowered into position inside the airship as she began to grow.

The main frames of the airship were fully stressed, designed to be rigid without depending on wire bracing - and so an unusually complex structure was needed, with the result that the weight of metal used was more, in proportion, than that in the earlier airships, and much more than that in the R. 100, which was nearly as large. And, as we have already said, where metal of two thicknesses could be used for any part, the thicker and heavier gauge was always chosen in the interests of safety.

On 2 October, 1929, the Air Ministry escorted a party of Press representatives over the Royal Airship Works at Cardington, and issued them with notes on the airship under construction. To forestall any criticism, these stated that 'if British designers had been content to follow closely the Zeppelin system of construction as practised in 1924, the new airship would have been finished long since; instead they proceeded to tackle the problems involved on new lines...' There was a further departure from German practice in the use of a relatively small number of larger girders as against Zeppelin practice of using a large number of small girders, because the Air Ministry insisted that the hull, as constructed, must be capable of being stressed mathematically. As a result of the designers' refusal to follow the German system, the actual construction of the airship took four years, plus about two years of preliminary work.

In a lecture that Colonel Richmond gave in 1930 he discussed various points that might be incorporated in airships of the future, and remarked that certain fish, noted for their speed, such as the tunny, the porpoise, the swordfish and the blue whale, had shapes very like those of airships. He declared that 'it was not outside the bounds of possibility that either by the emission of an oily substance or by the presence of scales or by the nature of flow through his gills, the fish manages to prevent a smooth flow from becoming a turbulent one.

'It is possible,' he went on, 'that in years to come, the outer covers of airships may be provided with something in the nature of scales or feathers, or special ducts leading air from the nose of the airship to escape out of various points on the body, but at the moment, these are put forward as interesting speculations rather than as of immediate practical use.'[2]

In fact, the R.101 had such ducts, and they were essential, because they ensured that the air pressure inside the envelope was the same as the pressure in the atmosphere through which the ship was flying; if it varied significantly, then the fabric sides would rip. The gas valves were designed to deal with a maximum rise of 4,000 feet a minute - a speed of 45.5 miles an hour - and such a speed would mean that considerable differences in the air pressure could arise on both sides of the envelope. A number of slits were therefore cut in the nose, with others towards the tail, so that the air, having circulated around the gasbags, could then be exhaled. These vents were very ingeniously designed, but they had the weakness of allowing the entry of rainwater, as Lieutenant-Commander Atherstone, the First Officer, continually pointed out. Should this water reach any of the gasbags in quantity there was a danger that the goldbeater's skins, which were very vulnerable to damp, would become mouldy and porous.

In the early days all these innovations were tested zealously, and sometimes to destruction. To discover what stresses the components of the airship might have to suffer under different conditions, a complete section was set up and weights of up to six tons hung in various positions to see how it stood the strain. It survived triumphantly, and also passed a further test without any weights but with a gasbag inside to reproduce a certain type of shearing stress. For these tests one face of the section was attached to the end wall of the great shed at Cardington and all other supports were removed.

In addition, various experiments were carried out both in England and in India concerning the method of treating the fabric that would cover the frame. Colonel Richmond maintained a personal interest in all this, for during the war he had devised a new type of doping for the balloons, and an American company, interested in developing balloons, applied to buy his invention, but because he was a serving officer the Air Ministry refused him permission to dispose of any rights. The American concern then asked whether the position could be reconsidered if America came into the war. Whatever was agreed when America finally joined the Allies did not benefit Colonel Richmond, who received nothing material from his idea. He did receive something that he probably valued far more; the nickname of 'Dope' Richmond. Many others in the airship service also had nicknames: 'Bird' Irwin, the R. 101 Commander; 'Sky' Hunt, the Chief Coxswain; and 'Shorty' Short, the Chargehand-Engineer. They were a mark of their popularity and also a reminder of the friendliness of a small service.

In previous airships - and in the successful Zeppelins - the canvas had been stretched over the frames and then sprayed or brushed with dope. Under this new scheme the fabric was doped first and then stretched over the girders in the belief that it would thus be both lighter and tighter, for one of the great disadvantages of fabric as an outer cover was that it stretched easily and then would flap like a loose tent wall. In a strong wind it could tear very quickly, as happened to R.100 on her voyage to Canada in the summer of 1930, although her performance was unaffected. The idea of doping the canvas first was not successful, for the fabric appeared to absorb moisture, and consequently to shrink and rot, and shred. It had also been hoped to minimize flap further by pulling in the panels of fabric by long strings, which were joined to the fabric by some kind of rubber solution. This had a strong chemical reaction with the dope and rotted the fabric. Eventually the whole envelope had to be stripped off and replaced with new canvas which would be doped in the conventional way. The ship contained miles and miles of girders against which the fabric was stretched and to make sure that not a shred remained was a most formidable task.

Nevil Shute remembers visiting Cardington some time afterwards and seeing Squadron-Leader Booth, the Captain of R.100, with another officer, examining a small part of this tattered linen.

'In parts it was friable, like scorched brown paper, so that if you crumpled it in your hand it broke up into flakes. I stared at it in horror, thinking of R.100. "Good God," I said. "Where did this come from?"

'"All right," said Booth. "That's not off our ship. That's off R.101!"

'I asked, "But what's happened to it? What made it go like this?"

"There was nothing that he or I could do about it. I said, "I hope they've got all this stuff off the ship."

'He smiled cynically. "They *say* they have." '3

Booth, now a Wing Commander and retired from the Royal Air Force, remembers the incident well. It has stayed in his mind, because he believes it is possible that some tiny part of this ruined fabric remained on a high girder, and in the storm that raged during the airship's last flight this weakened fabric tore and let in the rain. But no one will ever know for sure.

Another innovation concerned the steering. The huge vertical and horizontal tail fins - the rudder and elevators that steered the airship and brought her up or down - were controlled by two ship's-type wheels in the control car. One man, the steering coxswain, worked the rudder and another, the height coxswain, controlled the elevators, and it was a measure of the vastness of the whole airship that each moving flap had a span of about 44 feet. Such an enormous area was believed to be hard to turn in a strong wind (although calculations for the R.100 had proved that they were not) and so a servo motor was provided to move them, just as a similar motor helps to apply the brakes in a high-powered car. The machinery for all this, which included a Vickers-Janey Variable Speed Gear, was fitted in the bottom fin, but even so all the elevators were arranged so that in an emergency they could be worked by hand. No servo-motor was built into R.100, for it was felt that such a motor was unnecessary and would be just so much extra weight and something else to go wrong.

To provide for the long range needed in an Empire service, R.101 carried 38 main fuel tanks each holding 224 gallons, and some of smaller size. Several were also arranged on the passenger decks, so that they could supply a compensating weight when the full complement of passengers was not being carried, or when passengers were disembarking, and these could, of course, also increase the airship's range if she were flying on some unusually long flight without any passengers at all. If all these tanks were filled, she would have roughly 37 tons of fuel aboard, or 10,000 gallons. If the airship had to be trimmed for weight in the air, compressed air could blow fuel from any tank into a central pressure tank from which it could be channelled at will to any other tank.

In 1927, after more than two years of design calculations, work began on translating theory into an airship. This occupied a further two years, so that it was September 1929 before R.101 was ready for her early tests.

In the summer, before the R. 101 ever came out of her shed, Professor Bairstow and Professor Pippard were invited to examine the calculations that Colonel Richmond and his men had prepared with a view to making their own independent report on the airworthiness of the airship. On Guy Fawkes' Day of that year - the date on their report - they noted: 'We do not see any such danger as would render the airship unairworthy for the trial flights; during these flights, experience will be gained on which the grant of a Certificate for overseas use can be decided.'

The few trial flights she made were covered by a temporary 'Permit to Fly', which was issued after the report had been studied and following periodical inspections by the Air Ministry's inspection department. First of all, however, before any flight at all could be made, she had to undergo a 'lift and trim' test in the huge shed at Cardington. This meant that the gasbags were filled with hydrogen so that they could measure her 'useful lift' - the amount of weight of passengers or goods she would be able to carry on any voyage. Here came the first setback, the first suspicion that all was not as well as had been hoped, for instead of having a useful lift of 60 tons, which was the amount intended originally, she had only a little more than half this lift - about 35 tons. This was due to the fact that her own weight had originally been calculated at 90 tons, an estimate that proved to be too conservative, for she actually weighed 113 tons, 12 cwt. The extra weight was accounted for by the engines, which were much heavier than had been anticipated, and also by the mass of extra equipment, such as the servo mechanism in the tail, which although ingenious, was belatedly found to be very heavy. With such a low margin of lift no long-distance flights could be contemplated with confidence, and a flight to a hot climate was quite out of the question.

Although this problem was one of some concern to the designers, there was cause for thankfulness that the airship was finally completed and ready to take the air at all, for she had been so long a-building that just to have her fly was a considerable achievement.

There was still a further delay, however, and although hotels in Bedford and round about were doing a considerable business putting up people who had come to see R. 101 make her maiden flight, sixteen days passed after she had been pronounced fit for flight before she actually took the air. This delay, which provided critics with further ammunition, was caused by the weather. It was too gusty, and no one dared risk the possibility of any mishap when she was finally taken out.

The airship was so large that she almost completely filled the shed where she had been constructed; there was a clearance of barely 25 feet at each side and about 10 feet at the top. The R. 100 had fitted her shed at Howden even more closely; she had only about two feet to spare on either side.

Should a crosswind spring up when the R. 101 was half out of the shed, then the working party who had to 'walk' her out, holding on to ropes suspended from either side, would not be able to hold her, and disaster was likely. What the Air Ministry wanted was a south-westerly wind which would run harmlessly through the shed instead of cutting across it.

'You cannot get that wind simply by issuing an order,' an official explained. 'You have to be patient. Our demands are no more exacting than is always the case with high-speed aeroplanes, which require a wind not stronger than ten miles an hour and visibility from the air of ten miles. There is no reason whatever for alarm, we simply do not want to take a gamble.

'R. 101 has 101 reasons for not being rushed out of her shed.'

The working party, consisting of 200 employees from Cardington, 150 airmen from the RAF station at Henlow, and 50 unemployed from

Bedford were kept ready, and at last, at dawn on 12 October, 1929, the world's greatest airship was taken out of her shed for the first time. Everyone remotely concerned with her construction, with their friends and relations, turned out from their beds to see her, and as she emerged slowly from the great dark archway, the early-morning sun turned her silver bows to pinkish gold, and a tremendous cheer went up. Two boys who had hitch-hiked from a village twelve miles away, but who never imagined that they would see the airship close to, succeeded in doing so by volunteering to carry a Press photographer's gear. They still remember this visit as a landmark in their lives.

The wives of the airship men were naturally out in force, for this was the supreme moment towards which their husbands had worked for so long; the reward for years of night-shifts and early rising, of hurried meals and work brought home. Mrs Gent, wife of the Chief Engineer, was almost moved to tears by the pride and magic of the moment.

'Here she comes!' she cried excitedly, clutching the arm of Mrs Scott, wife of her husband's Chargehand. 'Oh, what a beautiful sight! I wonder what she'll have done in a year from now?'

Exactly a year from then, to the very day, the bodies of passengers and crew who had died on her inaugural flight to Egypt were being buried in a mass grave at Cardington.

Two days after being launched, the airship made her first trial flight, and flew round Bedford for five and a half hours, for most of that time on two engines only; there was some trouble with the others, apart from their gross weight, which was 5 tons 16 cwt heavier than had been expected. No one who saw the silver vessel overhead had any idea that all was not well, and there was so much excitement that teachers led schoolchildren out into their playgrounds so that they could see the mighty airship pass above them in the autumn sky.

On 18 October the airship went farther afield, and stayed airborne for nine and a half hours, running on all four engines - for the fifth at that time was still being carried for reversing purposes only. The weather was good on both occasions, and Colonel Richmond, although he made no written report of the airship's handling, noted in his own diary that he was satisfied with the way she responded to the controls and with her general stability.

Lord Thomson made his first flight in the airship on this journey, and when he came down from the mooring mast afterwards, he spoke to reporters and told them of his hopes that he might be able to fly to India at Christmas in her. But again he stressed that he did not wish to bring any pressure to bear on the technical staff to undertake any journey until they were satisfied that everything was in order, and until they themselves were ready to leave. His policy would be one of 'Safety First'. A week later, in a Minute, he wrote: 'The right policy to pursue is to go on steadily with the progressive experiments and thus enable the full results of our extensive programme to be achieved. I do not anticipate any difficulty arising from weather conditions in the future if a slow and sure policy is insisted on from the first.'

Before they could make a third flight, the Meteorological Department gave warning of a storm that was approaching Bedford, and lest the airship should be damaged, she was hastily put back into her shed, and there she remained until 10 November. The complicated procedure of 'walking her out' again showed how difficult it was likely to be for lighter-than-air machines to keep to regular time schedules than orthodox aeroplanes. First of all, starting at dawn, the usual working party took 20 minutes to walk her out of the shed and attach her to the end of the mooring mast cable; and then they waited with her until a quarter to eight, when temperature conditions were judged suitable for her to be moored. Two hours later she cast off with Sir Samuel Hoare as the most distinguished passenger. As Secretary of State for Air in the Conservative Government he had contributed greatly to the airship's programme, and reporting this flight, *The Times* noted approvingly that, 'he may, therefore, justly claim to have played a big part in the results now being achieved, though R.101, of course, owes its existence entirely to Lord Thomson and the Labour Government, who, wisely, as events seem now to show, decided to institute two parallel lines of experiment rather than leave airships as a monopoly in the hands of one group'.

The wisdom of this decision is now a matter of history.

Before this flight was scheduled, the Air Ministry sounded out the Private Secretary to King George V about whether the King would approve of a flight over Sandringham, where he was then in residence, and had received permission for one to be made. Although the King was far more interested in naval matters than aviation, he was not without curiosity about this airship, for the Prince of Wales had visited Cardington to see her under construction and had actually flown in an airship as long before as 1913. By half-past eleven in the morning, R.101 was droning over Sandringham at 60 miles an hour. The day - like every day when the airship was taken out - was fine and sunny, and the sunlight caught the silver hull so that it glittered like a mirror in the sky. The King and Queen stood on a gravel path near their house looking up at this aerial manifestation of their country's pre-eminence, as Major Scott, who was in command, turned the huge dirigible in three wide circles at a height of 1,500 feet above them. As the airship flew out over King's Lynn, steamers sounded their sirens in salute. She turned over Cromer and then flew above the chimneys of Sir Samuel Hoare's country house before heading for Norwich, where dozens of workmen from Boulton & Paul's firm came out to cheer the passing of the giant they had helped to build. A small aeroplane actually took off from the company's airfield and flew alongside R. 101 in salute, like a pilot fish before a shark, emphasizing the airship's size.

It was then that someone remembered a remark that Dr Eckener, the Zeppelin designer, had passed about R. 101 when he had been shown the original drawings.

'Very nice,' he said slowly in his precise Teutonic way. 'But -isn't it a little big?'

1. *Empire of the Air* (Collins).
2. *The Development of Rigid Airship Construction.*
3. *Slide Rule* (House of Stratus, 2000).

CHAPTER FIVE

Work to Do

In the month when the R.101 was launched, at a time when recrimination seemed out of place, a sharply discordant note was sounded in a book by Sir Dennistoun Bumey. Since Burney had sown the seed from which both the R.100 and the R.101 had germinated, he spoke with authority and experience and his opinion commanded respect.

'As a result of the last seven years' investigation and work upon R.100,' he wrote, 'I am firmly convinced that airship enthusiasts not only overstated their case, but failed to realize that a vessel that could neither make a landing without elaborate extraneous aid, nor be housed or rigidly secured in rough weather, must always remain a doubtful value for commercial purposes... The cruising speed of all airships is far too low for commercial purposes and should be increased to not less than 90 miles per hour... This would entail a further considerable increase in weight in the form of more powerful engines, more fuel, and a stronger hull structure to withstand the higher speed. This increase of weight must necessarily entail a corresponding increase in size and thus will, emphasize the handling difficulties... As these ships are today, the R.100 wants at least ten tons extra lift, and the R.101, 22.5 tons extra lift to make them commercial propositions upon the London-Egypt route at the low cruising speed of 70 miles per hour."

A further disadvantage received publicity when a party of MPs went on a short demonstration flight and were all alarmed - and some nearly thrown out of their seats - by a sudden lurch as the ship left the mooring mast. The crash that had so disturbed them all was only the airship's crockery breaking and cutlery falling from the tables, because of a poor distribution of ballast. Sir William Brass, the MP for Clitheroe, who was aboard, asked the reason for this sudden lurch, and was told that the ship had 'too big a lift on the bow'. After discharging ballast to right the ship they went on an even keel. More than a month previously, just after the launching, Atherstone reported to Irwin that the gauges in these ballast tanks 'are not satisfactory, and cannot be relied upon'. He urged that 'a simple form of contents indicator is required for *all* tanks so that the level of fuel can be *seen'.* This was vitally important because the Captain had to know how much water the tanks contained so that he could trim the vessel.

There is no record in Atherstone's logbook that such gauges were ever fitted.

This voyage was further marred on their return to the mast by the fact that, although the day was calm, with little wind, the crew took an hour to anchor the airship at the masthead. Had a strong wind been blowing, then it might have taken much longer, or could even have proved impossible, for airships were all notoriously sensitive to any maldistribution of weight, and would buck and rear alarmingly under such conditions.

Whereas a ship at sea is limited in her movements by the water that surrounds her, an airship is far more at the mercy of her element. An aeroplane flies fast enough to pass an air pocket with very little sensation to any passengers, but the airship, which at her fastest can travel at only a fraction of this speed, naturally feels air pockets more strongly; she drops and rolls like a ship that lacks the impetus to cut through a heavy sea but must dip and rise with the waves. And at such times it became unpleasantly clear how completely helpless both passengers and crew were in a dirigible; they were subject to far greater danger than in an aeroplane or a balloon. The pilot of an aeroplane can bale out by parachute; the commander of a limp balloon can control the release of gas sufficiently so that the balloon descends gracefully (if ignominiously). But the crew and passengers of a rigid airship weighing 100 tons had neither of these ways to safety, for they flew so low that the parachutes of the time - even if they carried them - would probably not have time to open.

Any tendency to roll was therefore alarming, and in the case of R.101, also extremely serious, because the novel gas valves with which she was fitted would open and release gas required to keep her airborne. The general view of her early trials, however, was that she had behaved satisfactorily, if not outstandingly, and this view was corroborated when she rode out a gale at the mooring mast. She was deliberately left there to see how she would handle, and although the average speed of the wind was only 35 mph, a maximum gust of 83 miles an hour was recorded, and R.101 emerged outwardly unscathed. The storm did,' however, show up a weakness that was to become more apparent as time went on: the fact that the gasbags, despite their ingenious and complicated wiring harnesses, could chafe against girders under such conditions. Wing Commander Colmore, the Director of Airship Development, reporting to the Air

Ministry on how she had survived the storm, noted: 'Beyond the entry of rain and a certain amount of chafing of gasbags due to the roll, no damage whatever was sustained.'

'Sky' Hunt also put in his report, which was rather more critical: 'In the case of numbers 3 to 14 bags inclusive,' he wrote, 'a very considerable movement from side to side was taking place on each flat end, as much as three inches to four inches, and at times the surge of the bags in a forward and after direction was considerably marked. Owing to the combined two movements, where the bags were touching or nearly touching the radial struts around main frames...the plates on top of the radial struts rubbed and chafed the bags, and in places such as Number 8 starboard fore end tore the bag 9 inches in a jagged tear. Number 8 thus became deflated to 60 per cent, and on inspection taking place it was noticed that on every roll the valves opened to the extent of a quarter to half an inch. The holes on top of Number 14 bag were caused by the bag bearing hard on O girder, where several nuts project, and combined with the movements of the bag caused punctures.' This O girder was the top girder in the airship, and to have the bags pressed continually against this was a grave fault, for the whole weight of the airship was then bearing down on them.

On 17 November, 1929, R.101 made what was afterwards called 'a magnificent flight' and which lasted for more than 30 hours, the longest time she was ever airborne. She set off from Cardington on Sunday at 10.35 in the morning, by one o'clock she was over Scampton, near Lincoln, and three hours later over Tyneside. At six o'clock she was seen in Edinburgh and by eight watchers in Glasgow saw the long glow of her lounge windows in the evening sky. At 9.15 she was above Belfast, and then she turned back and in the very early hours of Monday morning passed over the Isle of Man, and on to Blackpool, then down over Dublin and back to Cardington by way of Holyhead and Chester. In Scotland the weather was very bumpy, and on the English coast they ran into fog which thickened over the Midlands, so that at Rugby only the top of the 880 foot wireless masts could be seen. They therefore decided to return more quickly than had been intended, a manoeuvre that Major Scott carefully explained was in no way due to any defect in the airship. 'The fog gave us no trouble at all except slightly to curtail our trip,' he said. 'We did not want to land in fog and darkness, so we decided to return sooner than we first thought.'

Their average speed had been roughly 60 miles an hour and the only thing to go wrong on the journey occurred when one of the wire 'bridles' - that transmitted the lift of the gasbags to the frame - broke as they were about to land because the pulley round which it worked was too small for its purpose.

From then until the end of the month the airship flew at anchor in the sky, nose in to the mooring tower, an object of pride to all who saw her. She was 'walked' into her shed on 30 November and she remained there until the following June. Five days before she came down from the mast Lieutenant-Commander Atherstone reported to Irwin that 'the control car has...quite a lot of bilge water under the floor boards and there is no means of getting it out... The sorbo mat which was authorized by DD AD (Major Scott) about 20th October has not yet been supplied for the control car. Are we ever going to get it?' His logbook does not contain any confirmation that this mat was supplied, and although on the same day he reminded Irwin that the ventilating system had not been properly finished and that 'it should be carefully examined and all leaks and holes properly sealed off, there is no record in his book that this was ever done.

In the seven weeks from her launching, R.101 had flown on seven flights in excellent weather, and all save one in daylight, for a total flying time of more than seventy hours, and had behaved well on them all. In these circumstances, however, it would have been surprising if she had not.

Sir John Higgins, the Air Member for Supply and Research, described these mild tests in a Minute for Lord Thomson, and was careful to point out that 'before she gets a full Certificate of Airworthiness, R. 101 has yet to do a 48 hours endurance flight. There has hitherto been no suitable opportunity for this as we cannot run the risk of an endurance flight finishing in a gale.'

But when the time came for her to begin a voyage of 2,500 miles with the promise of strong gale weather within a few hours, no one in authority seemed to consider this a risk at all.

The few careful flights R. 101 had made showed that a very small amount of roll made the gasbags chafe against the frame, and in the words of a report made two days before Christmas: 'There appeared to be a good deal of movement of the gasbags and gasbag wiring when the ship was rolling at the tower, the hull appearing to roll round them. This caused a fair amount of chafing on the bag all round the inner ridge, and a lot of padding will be necessary. There is a clear mark on each bag where this has taken place, and it may be worthy of consideration as to whether the bag should not be slightly reinforced at this point...'

When the airship was inside her shed again and decently shielded from public gaze all sixteen gasbags were removed and searched for holes; fifteen were found to be riddled with them. One had as many as a hundred and three, mostly very small pinpricks where the delicate skin had been punctured against a rivet or a girder, for since the wires had been lengthened to allow the gasbags to expand, they chafed against the girders in innumerable places. In an attempt to reduce this rubbing, no less than 4,000 special pads were made and fitted at as many points where rubbing might occur.

Although this would obviously be a great improvement, it still did not solve the greater problem: how to give R. 101 more lift. The total available weight the airship could carry in ideal circumstances was only 35 tons, which meant that a journey to India, for which at least 25 tons of fuel would have to be carried, was right out of the question - with only ten tons available for passengers, crew, baggage and stores. Thus the giant airship, 732 feet long, 132 feet wide and containing five million cubic feet of gas, hung in her hangar, a paradox of ingenuity. All the brilliance of her design was in danger of being dissipated in supporting her own weight in the sky.

There were only two immediate ways of giving an airship more lift, either by pumping in more gas, or by lightening her. It was therefore calculated that if every possible cubic foot of gas was pumped into the gasbags, the wires loosened to allow the bags to expand to their limit, and every fitting not absolutely essential for the actual working of the airship removed, about six tons weight would be saved. Airship designers tended to think in terms of tons where aeroplane designers worried about pounds, and indeed this saving was considerable, but still nowhere near enough.

Then a third proposal began to gain favour, as it had with other earlier airships - always with disastrous results: that R. 101 should be lengthened. This would allow another gasbag to be carried, the lift from which would more than compensate for the additional structural weight. The gain from this extra gasbag, the seventeenth, was calculated at nine tons.

This solution had a serious disadvantage: all the stresses and strains involved would have to be calculated again - a formidable task, and one made vastly more difficult by the fact that the work would have to be done against the clock, for every alteration made in the airship further delayed the date when she could start on her first flight to India. They could either attempt what was called 'the demonstration flight' to India in March or April with the airship lightened, and some considered this to be feasible, or they could delay the flight and increase the lift of the airship by adding a new gasbag in a new bay. For any regular services her lift would have to be augmented in this way, and so it seemed better to make the airship as buoyant as possible while they had the chance. It should be possible, the experts agreed, for the R. 101 to reach Egypt in perfect weather conditions without this extra bay, but she might not be able to go on to India, and, in any case, the return journey presented grave problems because of the temperature. Accordingly, the Air Council decided that 'in order to avoid running any unnecessary risks it is better to postpone the flight to India until the lift of R. 101 has been increased by the addition of a section in the middle of the airship'. The cost of all these alterations was put at £21,000 for direct labour and material, £2,500 for the gasbag and £1,000 for additional canvas needed to cover the bay.

Sir John Higgins described these alternative proposals in a Minute to Lord Thomson on 30 November. A week later the Air Minister replied: 'I am of opinion that no good, and quite possibly some harm, might be done by a flight to India in the early months of 1930. The best course would I think be:

'(a) To make the various alterations you suggest...

'(b) To insert the extra bay

'(c) To make every effort for a flight with 55 tons disposal load to India and back at the end of Sept., 1930.'

Accordingly, almost as soon as the great doors had been shut behind the airship, she was steadied by guiding ropes which kept her suspended between earth and roof; and work began on lightening her. The complicated servo mechanism which had been so painstakingly installed to work the rudder and elevators was torn out of the tail, and every fitting that could be removed or replaced by something lighter, was investigated. Up on the top of the airship was a lookout position for one man, where, in wartime airships, a cockpit had been supplied for a machine-gunner. This was now removed, some tanks were also taken out, and bunks and other passenger equipment dismantled and removed. Even the glass panes in the windows of the promenade deck were replaced by celluloid sheets.

It was also suggested that to enable R.101's flight to India to take place in the following September, 'the additional bays should be inserted by the end of July'. This completion date was given because the Air Ministry was determined that, after these long years of building, R.101 should appear at the Royal Air Force Display at Hendon on Saturday, 28 June, so that the public (and the critics) should see for themselves how well she flew. Once she had been cut in two there might be further delays, so this complicated operation was postponed until after the Display.

Accordingly, she was brought out of her shed in the third week of June to prepare for the Hendon demonstration and for more gas to be pumped in.

The morning was fine but rather humid, and someone suddenly noticed that the canvas sides appeared to be ruffling as she flew at the masthead. Almost immediately a long tear appeared and grew to a length of nearly 140 feet between two panels on the starboard side. Should this develop further, and a wind arise, there was a very grave danger that the entire fabric cover would be ripped off and the whole airship would be nothing but a metal skeleton in the sky with all her framework and gasbags exposed. Emergency teams of riggers in rubber shoes were therefore sent up at once into the jungle of struts and braces with canvas patches and needles and thread to mend the tear while the ship rode at anchor, and while there was still time for such a temporary repair to be effective. As they worked, the wind increased and rain began to fall, but by half-past five that evening what passed as a weather-tight repair had been made. Next day the fabric tore again in a different place. This also was repaired, but by now it was clear that the entire fabric was unsafe, and a flight in this condition might well be disastrous.

The canvas had rotted because it had been doped before being fitted. Every shred would have to be stripped away and replaced with new fabric, which could be doped when actually in place, after German practice. This was quite impossible if the ship were to be ready for the rehearsal of the Air Display on Friday, 27 June. The repaired cover was therefore reinforced with some strengthening bands and a short flight was made on the Thursday to see how the airship responded. The weather was good, and the cautious journey only lasted four and a half hours; fortunately there was no wind and the fabric held firm. As they prepared to land, however, the Captain had to drop two tons of fuel oil from about a thousand feet to help to manoeuvre her. This was necessary because, when they left in the afternoon the day was sunny and warm, and the gas in the bags was hot and had expanded, so giving the airship an increased lift. But on their return in the late evening, the gas had cooled to the same temperature as the evening air, with a consequent loss in its lifting power. That this should be necessary in the relatively mild heat of a June afternoon in England did not augur well for an airship which was expected to endure the heat of a voyage to Egypt and on to India; nor did it add to the peace of mind of those who were going on the journey.

It was at about this time that the clash of temperaments, present for long in a friendly way, became sharper and more acrimonious than before. Major Scott, for example, was a man of brilliance and verve, but paid little attention to time or punctuality. Often he did not wear a watch and so was constantly late for appointments, a practice which grew increasingly irritating as it spread to others in the team. More methodical officers protested that memos were not read or acted on quickly enough, and sometimes remained for weeks unanswered.

The rift of temperament spread to the crew, who, as civilians, were not subject to service discipline. Once a rigger made a remark which an officer (already desperately worried by the delays and holdups) so resented that he replied with a clip on the jaw. The rigger complained, and the officer was actually awaiting a Court Martial when the trip to Egypt ended the affair.

'Bird' Irwin sensed the many undercurrents of feeling, and the growing tensions among his friends, and while he had his own doubts about the airworthiness of R.101 and the wisdom of flying her to India, he did his best to appear confident, although those close to him knew he was deeply concerned. Ralph Booth and he, although they captained rival airships, were great friends - so close indeed that when Booth took R. 100 to Canada, his wife stayed with the Irwins until he came back. Thus, all that summer, their two wives saw a good deal of each other, and on one exceptionally warm day they went off to Bedford together to swim. Halfway through the morning, Olive Irwin suddenly turned to Mrs Booth and asked her a question.

'Look,' she began a little diffidently, 'if by any chance Bird should get out of his ship, would Ralph volunteer to fly her instead?'

The question astonished Mrs Booth.

'I just don't know,' she said frankly. 'I've never thought of such a thing, but I'll find out and tell you.'

Some time later she asked her husband, as casually as she could, what his position would be if Irwin resigned his command.

'Just supposing for one minute that Bird was posted somewhere - or left - would you fly his ship? I mean, would you *volunteer* to fly R.101?'

Now it was her husband's turn to be surprised.

'I wouldn't get a chance to volunteer,' he replied shortly. 'I'd be ordered to fly her.'

There could be no other reply, for certain officers and men of each crew were already interchangeable, and if Irwin resigned there was no other airship captain in Britain so experienced as Booth to take his place. When the two wives met again, Mrs Booth told Olive Irwin what her husband had said.

The two women sat silent for a moment.

'Well, right you are, then. That's that,' said Mrs Irwin as brightly as she could. Neither of them ever referred to the subject again, although Mrs Booth has never forgotten it, nor the worry that had prompted the question.

At eight o'clock on the morning of 27 June, with the holes in the outer cover more or less patched up and the crew hoping that the weather would keep fair, R. 101 set off for the rehearsal of the RAF Air Display at Hendon. Flight-lieutenant Irwin was in command, as usual, and Ralph Booth was also on board for this trip, interested to see how the behaviour and performance of the airship compared with his own. He was standing in as First Officer, for Atherstone had left for Canada with the mooring party in preparation for R.100's flight there the following month. Booth was not, in fact, greatly impressed by R.101's handling, but attributed the unusual bumpiness of the flight to the fact that they were flying at only forty knots.

The highlight of the Display was for the R. 101 to come in over the crowds and then dip in a royal salute above their heads. This would indeed be a most impressive sight to see, but to be effective it had to take place at a fairly low level, which would not be a very safe undertaking with a vessel nearly 250 yards long. As they approached Hendon Aerodrome, Irwin ordered the height coxswain to bring her down into a gentle dive. The man spun the wheel, and the airship dipped rather lower than Booth considered necessary, until she was within 500 feet of the ground.

Irwin gave a second order: 'Bring her up now, height coxswain,' and again the wheel spun, for at this altitude there was danger of the airship actually scraping the top of a hangar. The airship responded, however, and rose steeply, and at that moment came a crack like a gunshot and a jerk in the control car as though something had broken amidships. The officers looked at each other, wondering what it could be.

'I'll go and see what's happened,' Booth told Irwin, and ran up the companionway to the main control car where a duty rigger explained that one of the main wire bridles had broken -just as it had broken on the tour round Britain the previous November. Later, these wires were replaced by chains, for greater strength.

The height coxswain reported that the airship was difficult to keep up at Irwin's flying height of between 1,000 and 1,200 feet, and during the day Booth noticed with concern that nine tons of ballast were released. As they had used two tons of fuel for the outing this meant that when they returned they were eleven tons lighter than when they had set out. The need to shed so much ballast could only mean that the ship was losing buoyancy because gas was leaking from the gasbags at a most rapid and alarming rate.[2] Booth drew Irwin's attention to this, but Irwin seemed to think the gas valves were giving trouble because of the slackness of the outer fabric cover. This was flapping furiously throughout the flight and could not be pulled in more tightly because of its condition.

The airship was 'flying heavy' - which meant that had she been stationary in the air the gas in the bags was just not sufficient to support her weight, and she would have fallen slowly to the ground. In spite of this condition, Irwin could still keep her flying for a short distance by a judicious shedding of ballast to keep up the bows and by using the elevators to hold her steady.

Captain George Meager, First Officer of R. 100, watched from his home at Sandy, Bedfordshire, as R. 101 came back, and later remarked on the way she was pitching. He spoke to some officers who had flown in her before but they replied that 'she always did it'. Next day, for the flight to Hendon for the actual Display, Meager travelled as First Officer, and was on watch on the journey back to Cardington. The airship suddenly began to dip into a sharp dive, and then started a long slow climb back as the height coxswain struggled to bring up her nose. Meager thought she seemed unusually heavy and remarked on this to the height coxswain, whose face was streaming with sweat in his efforts.

'It's as much as I can do to hold her, sir,' the man replied, so Meager at once ordered half a ton of ballast to be discharged, but still the airship felt heavy, and as they were not far from Cardington he suggested they should make for home immediately. Irwin was not so sure that this was wise, for the weather was bumpy, and doubted whether conditions were suitable for getting on to the mast, so they cruised about a little longer and finally came in two hours later.

By this time R. 101 had flown for a total of 102 hours, but the longest flight had only lasted for 30 hours 41 minutes, and all had been deliberately made in mild or sunny weather; 'very perfect flying conditions,' as Colonel Richmond called them in his diary. The only time the airship had met bad weather was when she lay at her mast and rode out a brief storm. Thus, she was virtually untried in general flying conditions, and consequently no one felt over-confident about her performance or her capabilities for a long flight East.

As long before as on 22 January, in a letter to a friend, Colonel Richmond had written that...'a 5,000,000 cubic feet airship, according to current British ideas, is not suitable to carry 100 passengers for journeys to the East at all times of the year... Either we must have our stopping places closer together or our airships larger, or both...'

Wing Commander Colmore had already been pressing for additional emergency mooring masts to be set up on both legs of the journey East; at Malta, for the first part, and at Baghdad or Basra for the second, but nothing had been done, nor was anything ever done about such intermediate staging posts. A few weeks previously, Lord Thomson, in a debate in the House of Lords on Civil Aviation stressed that: "This is one of the most scientific experiments that man has ever attempted, and there is going to be no question of risk -

while I am in charge - being run, or of any lives being sacrificed through lack of foresight. It is far too scientific and important a matter for that...'

This was his public opinion, but when on 30 June Sir John Higgins told him that the airship should be ready by 21 September, and that there would be one trial flight, he replied: 'I should like to be able to count definitely on starting for India during the weekend of 26-28 September. I ought to be back by 16 October...'

Flight-Lieutenant Irwin meanwhile was reporting to Major Scott that 'during flight...the outer cover...was flapping considerably more than on previous trials... It is considered possible that gas valves may have been affected, as even allowing for the numerous holes which are now being found in gasbags where they have rubbed on protruding nuts of Main Longitudinals, the loss of gas would not have accounted for the heaviness of the ship during flight on Friday and Saturday...'

Colonel Richmond also had something to say in a note to Major Scott on this disturbing loss of gas: 'In connection with the reported loss of lift of R.101 during flight, I have been investigating the effect of holes in the gasbags. I find that, if it be assumed that the average height of the holes is equal to three quarters of the height of the ship, then the rate of loss of lift is about one ton per square inch of opening in 12 hours. This calculation assumes quite a pessimistic co-efficient of discharge...

'In my opinion, this result is somewhat startling and emphasizes the great importance of guarding against holes in these present ships. In order to enable me and my staff to determine what should be done to check holes...and also to guard against their recurrence in future ships, I should be glad if you could arrange to let me have full particulars of the positions, approximate sizes, etc. of the holes found by the crew, from time to time...'

Colmore and Richmond also discussed this constant loss of gas, for it was probably the most serious threat to all their work. Clearly, if the ship could not stay up in the air because of escaping gas, then all their ingenuity would be lost, for there was a limit to the amount of ballast and equipment such as bunks, that could be ripped out, and already the airship had been denuded of many of its more luxurious fittings. If this process of 'adding lightness' was pursued, they would soon have a great empty shell 250 yards long that could cruise uselessly through the air carrying only her crew in spartan surroundings, a worrying prospect. Sharing the officers' concern was Mr F McWade, the Inspector in Charge of the Aeronautical Inspection Directorate at Cardington, and the man who, in the last analysis, would have to issue - on behalf of the Air Ministry -the certificate of the airship's airworthiness, and the Permit to Fly. He was so disturbed that on 3 July he decided to write a strong memo on the whole subject, and rather than send it through the usual channels, where it would be passed from hand to hand through the slow hierarchy of his Directorate, he took the most unusual step of sending it direct to the Secretary of the Air Ministry, then at Adastral House, in Kingsway, marking it 'For the attention of the Director of Aeronautical Inspection'.

It was headed 'Confidential' and then: 'HMAR.101. - Airworthiness of the above ship.'

He wrote: 'On the 26.6.30 I handed over the "Permit to Fly" dated 20.6.30 - valid until 19.7.30.

'Owing to the modifications which have recently been carried out on the Wiring System, the gasbags are now hard up against the main longitudinals and rubbing very hard on the nuts of the bolts positioning the stirrup into which the tie rods are screwed. Further, the gasbags foul very badly the heads of the taper pins at the points of the main and intermediate struts at the inner ridge girder ends. This matter, in my opinion, has become very serious, as the points of fouling occur throughout the ship and amount to thousands.

'Padding has been resorted to by wrapping fabric over the parts mentioned above and this is the usual recognized method used in isolated cases. Padding to the extent now necessary is, in my opinion, very unsatisfactory, because the bags move when the ship is in flight and the padding becomes loose and the projection complained of is again exposed. Although the gasbags have recently been reconditioned and were in good order when placed in the ship a few weeks ago, there are now many holes in them.

'The next point is that where the fabric is wrapped round a joint it may be difficult to know what is happening underneath the wrapping. I have in mind the corrosion question. The fabric will become damp and in many cases wet when the ship is in flight; therefore, there will be alternate process of wetting and drying of the fabric which must be detrimental to the metal underneath.

'I am fully aware that to remedy the faults complained of is in the nature of a large undertaking and it may be necessary to remove the bags from the ship. Until this matter is seriously taken in hand and remedied I cannot recommend to you the extension of the present "Permit to Fly" or the issue of any further permit or certificate...'

The Director of Aeronautical Inspection, Colonel H W S Outram, at once got in touch with Wing Commander Colmore, and explained that he would have to pass Mr McWade's note on to Sir John Higgins, the Member of the Air Council who dealt with such matters. Before he took this step, however, he would be grateful for Colmore's own comments on it.

This put Colmore in a difficult position, for unknown to McWade, Lord Thomson had just written the Minute stressing that he 'ought to be back by 16 October'. So if Colmore agreed that the position was as serious as McWade claimed, then the R. 101 might be refused a Permit to Fly; their work would face a further humiliating delay and all concerned would incur the Air Minister's displeasure. Of course, the position was serious, but then steps were being taken to remedy it; all would yet be well.

'I feel sure you will agree that we cannot accept, as a matter of principle, that the gasbags in an airship should be clear of all girders,' Colmore wrote reassuringly in his reply to Colonel Outram. 'Also I expect you will agree that we can accept padding as being a satisfactory method of preventing holes forming in gasbags from this cause. As far as we can trace at present there have been remarkably few nips in the gasbags of R. 101 and that the holes which have occurred are due to the bags fouling girders. We have little doubt that padding will be a permanent remedy and, if this is accepted, then it is certainly not a large undertaking to put the matter right. In fact, we hope to complete the necessary padding in R.101 by the end of the present week or, at any rate, some time next week. We do not think any objection can be taken to wrapping padding round obstructions of this nature.

The above covers our views but I should be glad to discuss the matter with you when you are next at Cardington.

This interchange provides an example of the unusual situation whereby when all the airship experts were working at Cardington, engrossed with their monster, while their titular superiors, at the Air Ministry in London, fifty miles away, were, as the Court of Inquiry later stated, '...almost without exception, men whose training and experience had been gained in the course of service with aeroplanes as distinguished from airships.' The Court of Inquiry's statement continues: 'When, therefore, questions arose...which are peculiar to airships, there was a tendency at the Air Ministry to rely upon the advice and judgement of the airship experts who were congregated there...'

This meant that the design and construction team working on the R.101, instead of being able to look for advice and council from outside experts in the Air Ministry, had indeed to advise them. It was ludicrous that they should be asked to criticize their own work, and inconceivable that they should do so.

Thus Sir John Higgins, the Air Member for Supply and Research, never received the letter which Mr McWade had taken such a liberty in writing. Afterwards, at the Court of Inquiry, when Sir John Simon expressed surprise that the note had not been forwarded, Colonel Outram explained: 'When I first received Mr McWade's letter I was very much concerned about it. I thought we were up against something very serious, but after I had actually discussed the matter with Colmore, and made other inquiries from McWade by telephone, I came to the conclusion that it was not so serious as I had at first thought...'

Instead, on 11 July, Colonel Outram wrote back to McWade, giving him his own views on the matter, and also those of Wing Commander Colmore, and adding: 'As you yourself realize, it is impossible to alter the hull structure of the ship at this stage. The only expedient at the moment is to pad. It is your duty to see that every point which may lead to damage is padded in a proper manner...'

It was, of course, precisely because there were so many points that could lead to damage that this good advice was virtually impossible to carry out - and why Mr McWade had written in the first place. He had sounded the alarm and no one had heeded him. There was nothing more he could do.

Work was now about to begin on the great surgical operation of cutting the airship in half; inserting a further section that would increase her length from 732 feet to 777 feet, and then sewing her up again. Colmore knew that if he were to have a fighting chance of successfully finishing this fearful operation in time to fly to India in

September he had to start at once. But this he was not immediately allowed to do, for political expediency.

The airship R. 100 was expected to fly to Canada, but although she had already taken a flying test that lasted for 53 hours, she still had to pass a further one of 24 hours continuous flying, for certain defects had become apparent in the last five hours of her long test. If she did not pass the second test, she might not be able to fly to Canada; and if her sister ship the R. 101 was lying in her shed cut in two pieces, the Government would have no airship at all to make this voyage, in preparation for which a mooring mast had already been constructed outside Montreal at a cost of more than £50,000. Sir John Higgins discussed this with Lord Thomson on 1 July. 'Rather to my surprise,' he admitted later, 'he said that if the modifications to R. 100 were not satisfactory, the flight to Canada could not be made, but nothing must delay the preparation of R.101 for the flight to India...' Two weeks afterwards he wrote to Lord Thomson: 'I propose, therefore, if you agree, to hold up work on R. 101 for a week in the hope that R. 100's flight will be completed by then.'

Lord Thomson was not too pleased at this further delay, and replied the same day: 'So long as R.101, is ready to go to India by the last week in September this further delay in getting her altered may pass.

'I must insist on the programme for the Indian flight being adhered to, as I have made my plans accordingly.'

Sir John sent a copy of this note to Colmore, who pointed out that, in such a complicated task as cutting a ship in two, 'delays may occur which cannot be foreseen', and he suggested that 'in the event of further trouble with R. 100 during her re-trial flight I am afraid the only alternatives would be either to abandon the Canadian flight until these troubles have been overcome or to carry out the flight with R. 101 and postpone the Indian flight until November.'

The ball was now back in Sir John Higgins' court; a place where he did not allow it to lie for long. On 21 July he discussed the matter further with Lord Thomson, and later that same day took the precaution of sending the Air Minister a note about it.

'1. I understand from our conversation this morning that you do not approve of the proposal that R.101 should be kept as a standby for the Canadian flight,' he wrote, 'and that if the modifications which have been made to R. 100 do not prove satisfactory, the flight to Canada will have to be put off until satisfactory modifications are completed on this ship.

'2. I propose, therefore, to issue instructions to DAD (Director of Airship Development) to part R. 101 immediately so as to give the best chance of its being ready according to the programme date which is being worked to.

'3. Every endeavour is being, and will be made to keep to this programme date but, as stated in my loose Minute of the 30th June, which I have inserted for reference at enclosure 5a, this date does not leave any margin for unforeseen circumstances...'

The Minute he enclosed had given 22 September as the completion date for the lengthening. It added that 'one trial flight will be necessary before the airship leaves for India, so the end of September is the earliest date on which the flight can commence. This leaves no margin for eventualities and assumes that the trial flight will be completely successful.'

Lord Thomson replied on the following day:

'The first paragraph of your Minute states the position correctly. I note and approve course of action proposed in paragraph 2.

'As regards paragraph 3, I am sure everything possible will be done and I am not unduly pessimistic.

22.7.30. T'

In this last expression of opinion, the noble Lord was by now one of the few men concerned with the airship who was not pessimistic. Nothing was wrong with R. 101 that full trials and time for modifications could not cure, but they were to be allowed neither. Work had to start at once on dividing the airship into two.

There was nothing new in this idea; in 1917, when the Germans wished to send a large consignment of supplies to their troops in Central Africa, they lengthened the airship L.57 by 20 feet amidships in two weeks at Friedrichshaven. But they were not working against the clock as they were at Cardington; nor was their task so involved, for while work was in progress on R. 101 it was decided to take the opportunity of modifying the engines as well.

Up to this date, the airship had been propelled by four engines when going forward, the fifth being carried as dead weight and only used for reversing. These four engines were inadequate to power the airship as vigorously as had been hoped, and when she was lengthened she would be even more sluggish. Two engines were thus to be adapted so that they could run in reverse, and then all five could be used to drive her forward, as had originally been intended. Some unexpected delay occurred in the arrival of new starting engines, but even so officials calculated that, by working non-stop, with day and night shifts, the engines could be fitted and the hull lengthened by the third week in September. Advantage of the airship's enforced incarceration was also taken to remove the panels of fabric that had rotted and to replace them piece by piece with fresh fabric which was doped when it was in place.

The actual task of dividing the hull was simplified by the airship's original construction. She was simply cut in two and so remained, with both halves floating in the air within her gigantic shed at Cardington. She was kept close to the ground by weights slung from her sides; these were added to or taken away as the changes of humidity and temperature affected her buoyancy. Each transverse frame and the longitudinal girders were held by pin joints, which were uncoupled. Then both halves were pushed apart, leaving just enough space between them for the new bay to be fitted.

'The speed with which the extra bay has been fitted is a tribute to the simplified method of construction,' declared a correspondent approvingly in *The Times*. The new bay was actually constructed on the ground under the gap, a comparatively simple process, since parts had been standardized, and it was rather like fitting a gigantic Meccano model together. In less than a fortnight the framework was ready and had been hoisted between the two halves of the ship; the first attachments of the longitudinals were made in 40 minutes. The work was very awkward to carry out in the confined space, but speed was essential, and as one team of men came off duty they were relieved by another. The urgency of the matter communicated itself to everyone involved, for they all knew in their hearts that no more delays would be tolerated, no more excuses would be accepted. The airship *had* to be ready to fly on time, and so she was. Despite the enormous amount of work involved in modifying the engines, lengthening the hull by 45 feet, stripping off all the fabric envelope and replacing it, R. 101 was ready to be 'walked' out of her shed again by 25 September. Unfortunately the weather was so bad that they dared not take her out until it cleared - which was not until 1 October.

Everything was being arranged on the assumption that the airship would fly to India, for Lord Thomson had managed to postpone the date by which he wished to return to London from 16 October to 20 October, and although there had not been any high-speed tests of her engines, this was not a very good time to mention the fact. The 'gassing and mooring party', twenty men under Lieutenant-Commander William Watt, had left for India on 17 August and were busy carrying out tests with a training balloon in Karachi in preparation for landing the R.101 when she arrived. They reached Karachi on 10 September, just four days before the entire crew of the airship were vaccinated and inoculated for the trip.

Day and night, from the time the airship was finished, a handling party stood ready at Cardington to bring her out. At last, at midnight on 30 September, they were stood down as the weather still seemed bad, but at five-thirty in the morning they were called for again in a hurry. The wind had dropped and the chance of bringing her out of the shed could not be missed. So that there should be no danger of her blowing away, 350 men of the Royal Airship Works were on hand and another 200 were sent for from the RAF Station at Henlow. They arrived late, and by the time they were out of their lorries, the R. 101 was already at the mast.

She had come out at six o'clock and within the hour was locked home in her cone like a gigantic silver cigar in the chill October sky. A message was sent to the Air Officer Commanding, Middle East: 'R.101 left shed this morning for mooring tower and will start this afternoon on trial flight. Subject to trial being satisfactory, earliest possible date for departure would be evening of 3 October.'

The first draft of the message read 'will start this afternoon on 24 hours' trial flight', but this was changed, for, early on the previous day, Wing Commander Colmore had been in touch with the Air Ministry to discover whether the 24-hour test which the airship should have before being granted a Certificate of Airworthiness could be shortened.

On 1 September Sir John Higgins had been replaced as Air Member for Supply and Research at the Air Ministry by Air Vice Marshal (now Lord) Dowding, an officer who, at that time, had never been up in an airship at all. Air Vice-Marshal Dowding mentioned that if the trial flight lasted for 24 hours this would interfere with an engagement he had with the Controller at the Admiralty, and when

Colmore suggested that the flight should be shortened, at once asked whether he made the suggestion on his own accord. Colmore replied that this had nothing to do with it; his reason was 'so that we may have a chance, if all goes well, of starting on Friday evening. We shall then have all Thursday to work on the ship as well as Friday.'

Thus Air Vice-Marshal Dowding was able to accompany them on their trial flight, which was made in good weather, but even so was not free from trouble, for the starboard forward reversing engine developed an oil leak. A new washer was fitted, but the work was done at night and the engineers could not get this washer quite home in the darkness. As the leak persisted the engine was stopped, and in case the port engine should be similarly affected, this was only run at half speed. They made two attempts to moor her after a run of only 16 hours 51 minutes, for the Captain was impeded by the fact that he had stopped two engines thinking they would not be needed again, and then found them very difficult to start.

Colonel Richmond noted in his diary that it was 'impossible to carry out full speed test owing to the early failure of the oil cooler in the forward starboard engine. Flying conditions were very perfect and under these conditions all other items in the ship behaved admirably.'

The airship had been out through the night and returned on the Thursday morning. Later in the day Colmore went up to the Air Ministry and again saw Air Vice-Marshal Dowding. As they were going into Lord Thomson's room Dowding, conscious of his ignorance about airships, suddenly said, 'You are my adviser, and whatever line you take with the Secretary of State I shall back you up.'

Lord Thomson wanted to know how the flight had gone, and Colmore explained that it had been 'quite satisfactory' with the exception of the oil-cooler failure and some other small things that needed attention. The purity of the hydrogen in two of the bags was also rather low.[3]

Thomson wanted to be away by Friday evening, but Colmore opposed this as it would not allow the crew to have the necessary rest before beginning such a long journey. Lord Thomson then suggested Saturday morning, but Colmore replied that he wished to cross France at night to get better air conditions; it was always more dangerous to fly over land than to fly across the sea and also, for the same meteorological reason, he did not want to reach Ismailia before sunset.

"You must not allow your judgement to be swayed by my natural anxiety to get off quickly,' Lord Thomson told him.

Air Vice-Marshal Dowding then reminded the meeting that the airship had still not attempted a full-power test and it was suggested that she should do one near home on the way to Egypt, and then she could return if the test was not satisfactory. But the written instructions to the airship omitted any mention of this. It was in any case a strange proposal that an airship, setting out on a journey of great length and strain, should dissipate her energies in a full speed test before she had gone a few miles, especially when the Air Minister and the Director of Civil Aviation would be aboard, for obviously the moral effect of failure would be considerable.

The two professors who had reported on the airworthiness of the R. 101 in the previous November had also been asked to do so again once the extra bay was in position. In issuing this invitation the Air Council declared that they would be guided by the views of these distinguished scientists when it came to be decided whether a Certificate of Airworthiness should be issued to the lengthened airship. Without this certificate it would not be possible for the flight to India to take place.

In September, the month before the airship was due to leave, Professor Bairstow raised a number of queries about the material that Richmond had given him to study, and the Colonel answered them. He and all the airship team at Cardington were more worried than they cared to admit, because if the airship was to undertake her final trial on 1 October, she had to have at least a Permit to Fly, and so short was time, indeed, that on 26 September Professor Bairstow gave his sanction for the necessary Permit to Fly over the telephone, and promised that his full report would be ready in time to issue the Certificate of Airworthiness. In fact, it was not completed by 1 October, but on that day Professor Bairstow wrote to the Air Ministry, explaining the delay.

'...We have examined the new information supplied to us by the Royal Airship Works,' he explained, 'and have satisfied ourselves that R.101 as now existing with its additional bay complies with the specified requirements of the Airworthiness of Airships Panel. The difference between the conditions of R. 101 now submitted and those of the original design on which our previous report was based, surprised us by their magnitude; the differences are not primarily a consequence of the addition of the new bay. A good deal of general thinking and comparison on limited information has been required...and we have not had time since receiving essential information from the RAW, to prepare a sufficiently considered written report. We are proceeding to put our first draft into final form.'

It never did go into final form, because the two authors were still engaged on it when the airship crashed. The fact that these two consultants were not given time to present their considered opinion as to the airworthiness of the elongated airship was not allowed to stand in the way of the issue of the Certificate of Airworthiness. On Thursday, 2 October, this was issued. It began: The Secretary of State for Air, having regard to reports furnished to him, issues the present Certificate of Airworthiness, dated 2 October 1930.' It was signed by the Deputy Director of Civil Aviation. It did not state what reports had been furnished.

During these last desperate weeks of work, Wing Commander Colmore had been placed in an unusual and unenviable position - one that was probably unique.

First of all, as Director of Airship Development he was stimulating the Government's airship programme; next, he was working on the actual construction of the airship; and thirdly, he inspected the work being done. Finally, he had the task of advising the Secretary of State on her safety and giving an opinion whether or not she was fit to leave.

He was a modest, quiet and stable man, and friends believe that this weight of worry was a heavy load on him, for he knew with what impatience Lord Thomson would view any further delay. He had every reason to hope that no other holdups would occur, for in the middle of the week before R. 101 was due to leave, with her new bay fitted and her other modifications completed, they had only one remaining available day to make an additional flight with a full-power trial of her engines to see how the lengthened hull reacted to the controls. Instead they had to spend that day cleaning and squaring up the ship, ready to receive her load of distinguished passengers. Thus R. 101 went out at dusk on Saturday, 4 October 1930, without ever having undergone a trial at full speed in her final state. Her officers and crew, some of whom had been on almost constant duty for the previous fortnight, went aboard exhausted.

Shortly before the airship left a friend called in to see Colmore at his office and to wish him well, and found him sitting at his desk, pensive and more quiet than usual. He asked him the reason. Colmore looked up at him.

'If the ship doesn't get back in time for the Imperial Conference,' he explained slowly, 'I understand that not only will there be no money for further airship work, it just won't be *asked* for.'

There was no need for them, or for anyone else, to speculate what this could mean to the thousands of people who for the past six years had been dependent directly or indirectly on airship construction for their livelihood. No need, either, to wonder what it would mean to all their hopes of a regular airship service - for an even larger airship was already being planned. Thus, on that Friday evening, as Lieutenant-Commander Atherstone, First Officer in His Majesty's Airship R.101, made his daily entry in his diary, he probably spoke for all his friends in R.101 when he wrote: 'It was decided this morning that the flight to India would not commence until 1800 hours tomorrow as it would be too much of a rush to get everything ready by this evening. Everybody is rather keyed up now, as we all feel that the future of airships very largely depends on what sort of a show we put up. There are very many unknown factors, and I feel that that thing called "Luck" will figure rather conspicuously in our flight. Let's hope for good luck and do our best...'

1. *The World, the Air and the Future* (Knopf).

2. It was afterwards calculated that R.101 lost 22,588 cubic feet of gas through leaks every 24 hours.

3. The more 'impure' - that is to say, diluted with air - hydrogen becomes the more likely is it to explode when near a flame or spark.

CHAPTER SIX
'G-FAAW a Pris Feu'

Slowly the airship headed south, gas hissing from her valves as she struggled for height, and the rising wind drumming on the fabric of her vast envelope. The weather was worsening every minute and the crew realized that R.101 was rolling more on this journey than on any previous trip. She had never been out in anything approaching a storm before, and Harry Leech, the Foreman Engineer from the Royal Airship Works, felt her pitch and roll as an overladen ship crossing the harbour bar. He reported the extent of this motion to Squadron Leader Rope, who had already been considering it.

'I don't think it's serious,' said Rope hopefully. 'She's bound to roll in this weather. Where are we now, anyway?'

They peered out of the misty window of the lower control car, wiping away the condensation of their breath on the glass. The R.101 was almost over Hitchin, and as usual the crew were confirming the navigator's reports visually. On many flights, courses had actually been plotted along rivers or railway lines, or even along roads because the altitude was always low and, but for the noise of the engine, they could easily have carried on a conversation with people on the ground. In the early airships it was quite usual to stop the engines and shout down through megaphones to people in the streets to ask them where they were. Visibility was bad on this Saturday but still the lights of cars and shops and houses were visible through the moving wraiths of cloud.

Leech had taken part in the previous flights of R. 101 and all the engine tests, but never had he felt such fierce motion as above the fading lights north of London. As one of the dedicated band who had worked with airships from the very early days of the war, he had years of experience to draw upon. Afterwards, out of the Service, and also out of work, he and his wife had trudged round the country trying to find any job in engineering that would carry a house with it. Times were hard and the future looked bleak until one day he read an advertisement in a local newspaper appealing for men who had had wartime experience with airships to return to Pulham and begin work on the development of future vessels. From Pulham, Leech went to Cardington. He knew more than most aboard about the capabilities of the vessel for he had helped to build her, as well as to fly her. Thus, while the long airship, buffeted by wind, and streaming with rain, lumbered south over the outskirts of Mill Hill, Leech remembered the difficulties they had experienced with resonance in the engine trials. He peered out of the window again in the direction of the forward engine, which had been hard to start, remembering the splintered propellers they had experienced during their trials, and finding no comfort in the memory.

For a time after the airship had disappeared from sight, some wives of the crew stared up at the place in the sky where they had last seen her. One of them, Gladys Key, sat on a milestone near a hump-backed bridge that crossed a little stream near the airfield, thinking of her husband, Tom, a Chargehand Engineer. They had been married for six years, and as she sat there, oblivious of the cold and the rain, she remembered other important occasions of her life when the weather had been equally bad. There had been a thunderstorm on her wedding day, and the start of her honeymoon; and another on the day they went in her husband's motorcycle and sidecar to their first home at Pulham. The weather then had been so atrocious that water had leaked into the engine and her husband had to push the machine up to their new front gate.

Nor were only the wives thinking of the great airship. At Chequers, Mr Ramsay MacDonald, the Prime Minister, admitted to a sudden feeling of inexplicable gloom as he sat down to dinner. He had agreed that Lord Thomson should return by 20 October, if possible, for Thomson had explained that he believed the air discussions of the Imperial Conference could be postponed until then. Thomson had so often dined there with him, and only a short time previously at the Prime Minister's table they had joked together about his elevation to the peerage. A footman addressed Thomson as 'My Lord', and Ramsay MacDonald suddenly burst out: Thomson, I never realized before what I'd done for you!' Lord Thomson often made jokes about his title, telling of the time when a boy of nine engaged him in an argument that amused him, and he had replied: 'You're a clever boy, my son. You deserve to be a Labour peer!'

Now there were no jokes at Chequers, for although the Prime Minister had been assured that nothing could go wrong, he did not share the popular confidence in the airship. Indeed, during dinner he spoke his thoughts, saying that although Lord Thomson, who was his oldest and dearest friend, assured him that every contingency had been provided for, 'Yet,' he went on, 'I am still uneasy. I confess that my apprehension for unlooked-for danger and disaster, ridiculous, no doubt, and admittedly without the smallest basis in personal knowledge of individual experience, will not be set at rest until I know for a fact that the great airship has safely arrived in India..."

Up in the airship's warm wireless cabin where the clock hands pointed to 8.21, the operator tapped out a message: 'Over London. All well. Moderate rain. Base of low clouds 1,500 feet. Wind 240 degrees (about West-South-West). 25 mph. Course now set for Paris. Intend to proceed via Paris, Tours, Toulouse and Narbonne.'

In the streets of London crowds were out, peering up against the driving spears of rain to see the airship pass. There was little enough to see: red and green pinpoints from the navigation lights, and a dim glow from the lounge and dining-room windows above them in the sky. Now and then as the wind changed, they heard the roar of the engines rising and fading as she headed south.

The stewards in the kitchen, white-coated, balancing against the twist and dip of the floor, hurried to and fro from the dining-room with practised speed. The beds had already been turned down and the warm lights glowed invitingly in the dummy portholes of the cabins. The six passengers might have little in common, save the fact that they were thrown unexpectedly together in the wintry skies, but they made small talk at the dining table, speculating about the speed of the vessel, whether or not the river below them was the Thames or the Medway, how long they would take to cross the Channel.

At half-past nine Irwin ordered a message to be sent to the Meteorological Office at Cardington, asking for a radio forecast of conditions between Paris and Marseilles with special reference to the wind forces and clouds they could expect. If the clouds were thick then the gas would cool and contract inside the gasbags; the airship would begin to sink, and he would have to shed ballast to hold height. Such conditions could be dangerous if they occurred over high ground, and although he was purposely avoiding the Alps he still would have to cross the edge of the Pyrenees.

After dinner, the passengers sat in the lounge, looking rather lost in the vast chill emptiness of the place, and soon moved to the smoking-room which, being smaller, was also warmer. The airship seemed to be travelling more slowly, which was indeed the case, for they did not know that she was already running on only three engines. Some miles north of London the oil pressure began to drop in the engine in the after car and the engine was stopped while they tried to find the fault. Arthur Bell and Joe Binks, the two engineers in charge, crouched together by the warm, silent diesel, with the storm beating on the thin cover of the car. The only way back into the airship was up the outside ladder and along a hatchway, a difficult task on a dry day for those with squeamish stomachs, and doubly hazardous in a storm when the airship was rolling so heavily and the rungs were slippery with rain.

At twenty-five minutes to ten the radio operator sent out a further message: 'Crossing coast in vicinity of Hastings. It is raining hard and there is a strong south-westerly wind. Cloud base is at 1,500 feet. After a good getaway from mooring tower at 18.30 hours ship circled Bedford before setting course. Course was set for London at 18.54. Engines running well at cruising speed giving 54.2 knots. Reached London at 20.00 hours and then set course for Paris. Gradually increasing height so as to avoid high land. Ship behaving well generally and we have already begun to recover water ballast.'

The ship was, in fact, behaving far from well. She was rolling and pitching like a barque in a storm - to such an extent that the Captain had found it necessary to take in more water for ballast to steady her, for water could be pumped round the airship from tank to tank, wherever weight might be most needed. The airship's weight had to be kept constant throughout the flight, otherwise she would tend to rise as her fuel was consumed, and so an ingenious system had been devised to catch rain, or water vapour, from the upper air. On the top of the great envelope a scoop caught the water which could then be directed through pipes and valves into the ballast tanks. The message was really important not for what it said, but for what it did not say. The fact that the Captain was taking in water showed that he did not consider the airship to be overloaded, even in such conditions of wind and weather. People who came out into the streets of towns and villages along the route for a sight of R.101 flying over, did not share this confidence. The clouds were thick now, and all they saw was a row of dim lights flying so slowly by that many were convinced she must be having engine trouble (as indeed she was). As she passed over Pett Level, near Hastings, one observer, Mr Reginald Cook, actually thought of warning the Dungeness lifeboat to keep a lookout in case of accident over the sea. He calculated that R.101 was not more than five hundred feet up and flying broadside on. Rain was falling more heavily as she shook off the lights of England and started across the Channel, and several people remembered the well-publicized words of Lord Thomson: 'She's as safe as a house -except for the millionth chance.'

The after engine was still not registering oil pressure, but now suspicion centred on the oil pressure gauge; perhaps it was faulty. Harry Leech and William Gent, the Chief Engineer in the airship, climbed down into the aft engine car to change it. This was the engine that Lieutenant-Commander Atherstone, in a memo the previous November, had warned Flight-Lieutenant Irwin was being smothered in sewage when the septic tanks were discharged during flight. Now, rain had washed clean the smooth metal egg of the nacelle; it glistened in the light of the lounge windows, and the stationary propeller shone like a rod of polished ebony. From the window in the car, Leech suddenly looked out and was surprised to see waves breaking in white clouds of spray a few hundred feet beneath him. 'We're pretty low,' he said. 'Have a look for yourself.' Gent peered through behind him. He whistled, for the water stretched as far as they could see, a deeper darkness than the night, split by the white caps of the waves; cold, lonely, desolate. Several times as they stared, the whole airship gave a sudden downward lurch, throwing them against each other, and then her bows came up as she rode the storm. In the tiny space of the engine car, where the huge engine took up most of the room, and the little wire-grilled inspection lights glowed round the walls, the engineers looked at each other, sharing the same uneasy thoughts. Up in the body of the airship, Arthur Disley, the electrician, went in to see the wireless operator in the radio cabin which adjoined the control room. From there the sea also seemed uncomfortably close and he was about to remark on the fact when Lieutenant-Commander Atherstone took the elevator wheel from the height coxswain. The altimeter read 900 feet, and Atherstone put the airship up to 1,000 feet before he handed back the wheel.

'Don't let her go below a thousand,' he said.

'Ay, ay, sir.'

At about this time, some passengers, who were also wondering at their low altitude and were looking out of the promenade deck windows, were surprised to see a flare blaze out over the dark and shining sea. It had been thrown by Squadron Leader Johnston, the

Navigator, a qualified Master Mariner who had served in the Royal Naval Reserve and the RNAS, before navigating Sir Samuel Hoare's flight to India and the Flight of the R. 100 to Canada. It was the custom in airships to drop calcium flares into the sea to calculate drift, but the sight did nothing to reassure them. Nor, as Squadron Leader Booth later pointed out, was there anything specially significant in Commander Atherstone taking over the wheel, beyond an implied rebuke to the coxswain for ever letting his ship fly at less than 1,000 feet. Even this altitude gave very little manoeuvring height for an airship 777 feet long.

In the smoke room, Lord Thomson and Sir Sefton Brancker sat comfortably in their wicker chairs with Squadron Leader O'Neill and Squadron Leader William Palstra, who represented the Australian Government. It was odd to savour a cigar in the middle of five and a half million cubic feet of hydrogen, and yet to be perfectly safe. Unknown to them, all round the smoke room, beyond the bulkheads and in the ropewalks that ran the whole length of the vessel, honeycombing her, the crew were inspecting the gasbags. They wore thick wool sweaters against the biting chill, and rope-soled canvas shoes, so that there should be no risk of striking a spark on any bare metal. These shoes were not popular, for the slightest smear of oil on a metal rung meant that they slipped and slid alarmingly, and the experience of being up in the echoing semi-darkness of a space which was as high as a cathedral and more than 250 yards long, was already alarming enough.

On every side the wires and chains that were slung round the gasbags and their pulleys creaked and then sprang tight with a great clanking of links as the airship rolled; the hiss and rumble of escaping gas through the throats of the valves sounded like elephants breathing in the darkness above them. The gigantic gasbags moved continually like living things as the air pressure changed. Now they would be huge balloons, glowing with a faint eerie luminosity in the dim height of the arched roof, so that a man could walk beneath them and see them suspended above like enormous pears. Then a change in pressure would bring them down, flabby and bloated, so that he had to thrust his way past them, while the damp, stinking covers, laced with the guts of bullocks, clung around his face like a fog. The inside of an airship was no place for a claustrophobe - or even for a man with imagination.

In spite of the excitement of the departure - which was itself the culmination of years of work and months of frantic overwork - and the subsequent reaction, no one appeared anxious to go to bed. It was as though, like mariners on some uncharted sea, still relying on the winds of heaven, the passengers and crew of the R.101 felt better able to deal with any emergency when fully clothed. The Channel crossing took them two hours, and as the airship turned south away from the sea and flew over the low flat fields of Northern France, another radio signal went back to Cardington: 'Crossing French coast at Points de St Quentin. Wind 245 true 35 mph.' St Quentin Point stands on the mouth of the Somme River, and is about sixty miles from Hastings, on a direct route to Paris. Johnston knew the route well; he had flown over it many times by aeroplane, but now the wind was increasing, a fact that was only made less ominous by the news that the engine was running again in the after car, after nearly three hours' work on it. The crew were operating a watch system of three hours on and three hours off and at 11 o'clock the watch was changed. The new watch would be on duty until 2 am on Sunday morning.

Gradually the passengers drifted off to bed, walking to their cabins with bodies braced to keep their balance along the rolling corridor. Below them, the engines droned reassuringly and the propellers glittered like spinning silver discs in the light from the lounges.

It was after midnight when the telephone in Mrs Richmond's home rang. Homer of Cardington, the Newfoundland dog that Colonel Richmond had given his wife some time previously and which they had named Homer 'because he'll give us as much pleasure as the poet ever did', looked up at her questioningly. Mrs Richmond had been reading by the fire.

'Hullo,' she said, lifting the receiver, not knowing who would be calling her at this hour.

'Hullo, Mrs Richmond, Cardington wireless room here,' explained the voice at the other end of the line. T thought I'd ring to give you the message we've just received from the airship. Here it is.' He began to read slowly.

'To Cardington from R.101, 24.00 GMT. 15 miles SW of Abbeville. Average speed 33 knots. Wind 243 degrees (that is WSW), 35 miles per hour. Altimeter height 1,500 feet. Air temperature, 51 degree Fahrenheit. Weather - intermittent rain. Cloud nimbus at 500 feet. After an excellent supper our distinguished passengers smoked a final cigar, and, having sighted the French coast, have now gone to bed to rest after the excitement of their leave-taking. All essential services are functioning satisfactorily. The crew have settled down to watch-keeping routine.'

'That sounds all right,' said Mrs Richmond in relief. 'It was good of you to ring me.'

Very glad I could do so. Now you can go to bed, Mrs Richmond, for we're going off the air here at Cardington. We'll be back again tomorrow morning, early though, and I'll give you another call at six just to let you know where they are. So until then, good night.'

'Good night - and thank you.'

Homer of Cardington thumped his long tail on the floor as she replaced the receiver.

In the main control car Mr M A Giblett, the airship's Meteorological Officer, was calculating what weather they could expect.

At thirty-six, he was already Superintendent of the Airship Services Division of the Air Ministry Met. Office. He had flown in R.100 to Canada, and had travelled to India, South Africa, Australia and New Zealand, to advise the governments of these countries about the proposed airship services. As he worked, the wireless was in contact with Croydon.

Thanks for valuable assistance,' she signalled after one o'clock. 'Will not require you further tonight.'

Croydon replied: 'Am remaining on watch.'

The wireless operator began to check their position by signals from Le Bourget, and at 1.45 on Sunday morning, an approximate cross bearing had been calculated by lines of intersection running from Valenciennes 80 miles to the northeast and from Le Bourget, 40 miles to the south. The airship was roughly a kilometre north of the landing ground at Beauvais, and this was confirmed from Le Bourget at nine minutes to two that morning, and acknowledged immediately.

'Le Bourget from airship,' came the answer from R. 101. 'Acknowledge. Thanks.'

At 2.7 am Le Bourget asked the airship for her speed and again at 2.13 am.

When there was no reply, the station operator asked twice: 'Do you receive me? Do you receive me?' and when no reply came to this signal, he asked Valenciennes: 'Have you anything from R.101 since 1.50?'

The answer came back in one word: 'Nothing.'

Minutes later Le Bourget discovered the reason, and, using the airship's registration number for the first time, sent the news round the world in four words. 'G-FAAW *a pris feu!*

At Cardington, the night-duty telephone operator was sitting in his small office reading a book, waiting for the hours to pass. Suddenly one of the small shutters dropped in front of his switchboard, indicating that someone was about to make a call. He looked up, wondering who could be telephoning at this hour, and saw with some surprise that the shutter bore the name of Flight-lieutenant Irwin. This meant that someone was trying to make a call from his office, but this seemed absurd, for his office was empty.

The operator pushed up the shutter, thinking that it had fallen out of place accidentally, and went on reading. At once the shutter dropped again. Puzzled, he put it up for a second time and even held it in place for a moment before returning to his book. As he did so the shutter fell for the third time.

By now some alarm was mixed with his surprise, and with another member of the staff he went along to Irwin's office wondering whether thieves had broken in. But the office was empty, and as still as a tomb. The rain had stopped outside, and the night was quiet. There was no wind. Nor had anything been disturbed: the telephone was in its normal position and had not been moved.

As they returned to the operator's office something made them check their watches. The time was seven minutes past two.

Harry Leech climbed back into the airship after his long tussle with the engine over the Channel. The oil gauge had been faulty; now the engine was running again. He washed, had a quick supper, and then sought out William Gent in the smoking-room; they were old friends. At about one o'clock in the morning, Flight-Lieutenant Irwin came in and spoke to them.

'I'm glad you've got that aft engine running all right,' he said. That could have held us up a lot. Well, we've got a busy day ahead, so I think I'll turn in. Good night.'

'Good night, sir.'

'Look here, Bill,' suggested Leech as Irwin left the room. 'You'll have all your work cut out at Ismailia when the Egyptians come aboard. I suggest you go to bed and get what sleep you can now, and I'll do the night watch. It'll give you some chance of a rest, anyhow. You've had a pretty full day of it.'

Gent looked grateful.

That's very good of you, Harry,' he said. 'Just have a look round all the engines first. They seem to be running all right, though I'm not too happy about the weather. But that's out of our control. Well, good night. See you in the morning.'

'Good night, Billy.'

Now that he was on his own, Leech leaned for a moment over the rail of the promenade deck, feeling the throb of the engines through his hands, sensing every shudder the airship made as the wind took her, for she was so long that the bows might be in the middle of a storm current, while amidships all was calm and the tail was being buffeted by other winds. He peered out through the rain-pocked celluloid windows trying to see any landmark in the dark forest beneath him. There was nothing; here and there a tiny light flickered like a captive star.

The weather was as inhospitable as it had been over the Channel. The wind took the airship, worrying her, shaking her, but all the time the subdued rumble came up comfortingly from the engines which he knew so well. He could tell from their sound so much about them; their revs, the throttle openings. The roar was reassuring for the aft engine seemed at last to be on form again, and in this weather the airship needed all the power she had. He walked down the empty companionway, where the lights still burned and the rain lashed the outer cover; the floor dipped and rose and creaked with the stress of the storm. He climbed down through the hatchway, down outside the main structure of the envelope, down the ladder suspended in mid-air to begin his tour of the engine-cars.

The Engineers, suspended in thunderous isolation above the sleeping countryside, imprisoned with their engines in their tiny metal globes, sought his eyes for reassurance, glad to see him, their faces pale in the throbbing light of the dynamo and the heavy, oil-laden atmosphere. The constant background bellow of the open exhausts made ordinary conversation impossible, and so the procedure was the same in each car: the raised eyebrows, the nod, the smile.

'Everything all right? Oil pressure OK?'

And the answer: 'Yes, sir. All's well.' They were good lads, all of them, he thought, as he clambered up the swaying, streaming ladder again into the momentary warmth of the corridor, and climbed down again on the other side into the other cars. Even if the engineers were isolated, at least their cars did not have the same claustrophobic atmosphere as the airship itself. For, luxurious and roomy as the lounge, smoking-room and dining-room might be, some could never quite rid their minds of the feeling of being hemmed in. Except for the hatches leading down to the engines, and the main entrance up in the bows, there was no way out. Passengers and crew were imprisoned in the airship's vast shell until the bow doors opened again.

It was nearly half an hour before Leech was finished, and the accumulated tiredness of the day suddenly swept over him; more than anything else he longed for a cigarette. His hand was feeling for a packet in his pocket when he remembered that he had none and that there was in any case only one place aboard the airship where he could smoke. Wearily he climbed the companionway to the smoking-room. It was deserted. All the wicker chairs were pushed back from the little round tables, as though a clutch of clubmen had left them unexpectedly. There were no windows, for reasons of safety, and the air was thick and heavy with the stale smoke of cigars, pipes and cigarettes. He sat down in a wicker chair near a table on which stood a soda siphon and a tray of glasses. Their rims touched and rattled as the ship rolled. Here, alone in the centre of the airship, surrounded by five and a half million cubic feet of explosive gas, but separated from it by the thickness of a metal safety wall, Harry Leech thankfully put up his feet and lit a cigarette.

Two o'clock, and time for the watch to change. In his bunk Joe Binks was still asleep, wrapped up in his fur-lined sleeping bag. High up in a corner of the crew room a light burned on the metal wall. George Short, Chargehand Engineer and Engineer of the Watch, came down the pitching passage towards him.

'Hullo, Joe,' he said, shaking Binks into wakefulness. 'What about it? Everyone's on watch save you. Ginger (Engineer Bell) is waiting.'

Binks groaned and stretched, gathering his thoughts, trying to postpone the agony of waking.

'Sorry, Shortie,' he said, and stuck his feet over the edge of the bunk, groping for his trousers and canvas shoes.

'Have a cocoa before you go,' Short suggested.

Binks shook his head. 'No, thanks,' he said. It would only delay him further, and he was late already. Short grinned, and held out the mug to him.

'If you don't drink it, I'll ram it down your throat,' he promised genially. Binks gave in, gulped the steamy brew, and then began to run down the ropewalk towards the trapdoor, through which he would climb down to his engine. The storm was now at its height and above his head the great gasbags surged and rubbed and squealed against each other in the darkness as if in a fury to be free of the restraining wires and out in the fearful sky soaring on and up to the stars. As he ran, Binks almost bumped into an officer.

'Excuse me, sir,' he said, as he squeezed past Squadron Leader Rope, who with Colonel Richmond, knew more about the gasbags than anyone else on board - for they had designed their valves and the harnesses that restrained them. His eyes were fixed on the gasbags, dim, monstrous shapes in the small glow of the working lights. Some time before he left Cardington Rope had jokingly told a friend who was worried about the gas leaks: 'If there's any trouble, don't worry. If need be, I'll spend the night up with the bags myself to see all's well!' Now he was keeping his word.

Farther on, Binks saw an engineer down on his hands and knees, trying to peer through the celluloid windows that were almost opaque in the rain. He paused, thinking the man was ill.

'What's wrong? What are you doing?'

The crouching man looked up at him.

'I don't know where we are,' he explained bluntly. 'I was trying to see the sea. I thought we were still over the Channel. But I can't see a thing, it's all so dark.'

As he spoke the airship rolled again, and Binks tore open the hatchway and began to climb down the ladder to the engine car.

'I'll always remember that night,' he said later. 'I'd got on a short duffel coat with wooden toggles and loops, and the wind was so strong that it ripped the toggles right off.' The breath was blown out of his body, and with the long rods of rain streaming in his face, blinding him, it was all he could do to hang on to the ladder. Mechanically he kept on going down, until his feet touched something more solid than a rung, and he felt the welcoming warmth of the engine come up through his thin shoes. He let go his hand and dropped into the car.

After the roar of the wind, the noise of the engine so close to him was deafening, and although he had a pair of earplugs -carried by all the engineers - he rarely used them because it was impossible to hear anyone speak.

Arthur Bell came round the polished side of the big Beardmore engine.

'You're late, Joe,' he began accusingly, jerking his head towards the engine car clock. 'Look at the time.'

It was four minutes past two.

'Sorry, Arthur,' began Binks. 'I overslept. I'd still be there now if it hadn't been for Shorty.'

'Well, I'm glad you're not. Look, now about this engine. She's been going fairly well, my watch, but keep an eye on that oil pressure.'

'Right-ho.'

Binks crossed to the small window and looked out. Suddenly he gave a cry of alarm. There, only a few yards away, was the roof of a church sticking up through the murk and rain like some huge and frightening mass of submerged rock in a celestial sea. It was the top of Beauvais Cathedral, one of the loftiest and most beautiful in all Europe.

'We're nearly at roof level!' he called.

'What?' shouted Bell against the thunder of the engine. 'I can't hear you! What did you say?'

'I said we're at roof level! I saw a church or something!'

This time Bell heard him and thrust him out of his way, peering through the window into the darkness.

'What do you mean? I can't see a thing. Are you all right?'

The two men stared at each other in alarm in the tiny overheated engine car, and then the airship lurched, dropped and recovered again. They staggered back, groping for handholds, anxious to keep away from the hot exhaust pipes. The airship righted herself, but Binks and Bell stood holding on to the side of the car, the breath beaten out of their bodies, for the sensation had been the same as falling a long way in a lift and then being stopped suddenly.

"What's wrong?' gasped Binks.

'Nothing,' said Bell. 'It's the storm.' But neither believed it. Then as they stood thus, glancing involuntarily at the oil gauges, their professional interest overcoming their personal feelings, the wind dropped unexpectedly. The airship was by now so close to the low ridge of hills outside Beauvais that she was sheltered by them, although no one realized this at the time. Binks peered out of the tiny window again, looking through the spinning blades of the small dynamo propeller towards the bows of the airship, sensing rather than seeing the vast hull just above them streaming with rain.

The floor dropped again and came up, but this time the rise was slower and more gradual, as though the great ship no longer had the resilience to rise to the challenge of the rain and the storm. Then she began to fall again.

'She's heavier,' said Binks. 'What's happening?'

Before Bell could reply, the telegraph rang for 'slow'. Bell immediately throttled back the engine. Neither of them could see anything but the dim silvery disc of the propeller blades shining in the light from the lounge; beyond and all round was darkness and rain.

But as they stared, trying desperately to see some light, some landmark, all their nerves taut with the thought of unknown danger, they felt the drum of running men along the ropewalks above them. The whole car trembled with the urgency of their feet.

Bell seized Binks by the shoulder, wondering if he had heard, and then, as he half turned, above the noise of running feet they heard 'Sky' Hunt's voice in a great roar of warning: "We're down, lads! We're down!'

In Shortstown, some of the wives were also passing a restless night. Mrs Hunt, the wife of 'Sky' Hunt, kept reliving the misery of that unhappy departure, and her forebodings, and those of her friend, Ida Potter, whose husband was also in the airship. At last, in the early hours, some inner restlessness made Mrs Hunt go to her window, which looked out over the quiet airfield. There was some comfort in the dim familiar landmark of the mooring mast, and then as she stood there she realized something was missing.

Usually, when the airship was due back from a flight, the mooring cone into which her blunt snout nestled, was left at the masthead. But now, because the airship was not expected back for at least two weeks, the cone was down. In this she read a portent of disaster; and went back to bed to endure a nightmare of uncertainty - until the new day brought it to reality.

It was warm in the smoking-room, if a little stuffy, but still very comfortable. Leech looked round at the furnishings again; the place was remarkable, and yet an illusion, for nothing was as it seemed. The walnut grainings and veneers were barely the thickness of a sheet of paper; the stout pillars, seemingly of oak, which supported the decorated ceiling, were hollow and so light that a child could have carried them. The new world of the air had not yet found its luxury and its style; this was the luxury of past days, of great ocean liners, of London clubrooms, of the world that had ended with the end of the First World War.

Leech lay back in his wicker chair, adjusting the cushion, listening almost unconsciously for the engines, enjoying the feeling that he had nothing to do now but rest and sleep. India; it was an exciting country to visit...

He put up his feet on another chair, feeling a little guilty about it, like a schoolboy putting up his feet in a railway carriage, and the droning of the engines almost lulled him to sleep.

A sudden shuddering jerk shook him into wakefulness. The floor was heeling over at an alarming angle and the light wicker chairs began to slide towards the bows. The roar of the engines came up more strongly for a moment and then the floor dropped level again. Leech swung his feet down, and at that moment the airship pitched again, so sharply that he was almost flung out of his chair. The soda siphon and some ashtrays on a table at his elbow skidded to the floor, and the chairs and tables in the room began to slide to the far bulkhead.

'Hello, we're for it,' he thought, and braced himself for the next dip or turn of the airship. In all his flights there had never been anything like this. He knew that they had been flying very low and that with each dip they must have lost a hundred feet. Unless they could gain height quickly they were in very real danger of running into a church tower or a factory chimney. As he waited, tense, leaning forward and gripping the arms of his chair, wondering which way the vessel would roll next, she dipped a third time and a tremendous shudder ran right through her, so that the floor and the walls trembled as though they were in an earthquake. Then there was a jerk and the airship stopped moving so abruptly that he pitched out of his chair on to the floor. At that moment the lights went out and he was alone in the darkness with chairs and tables sliding past him and crashing against the far bulkhead. The floor was at such an angle that he could not walk on it, but he half-ran, half-crawled to the wall and felt along it to the door.

He tugged at the handle, desperate to get out, but the handle turned uselessly in his hand and the door remained shut. The metal framework must have twisted as the airship came down. As he tore at the door, kicking it with his feet, flinging his shoulders against the panels, hoping that one would give, he heard the engine telegraph begin to ring with a note of fearful urgency, and then a roar as of a cataract of water, or the thunder of breakers on the beach: the noise of five and a half million cubic feet of hydrogen taking flame. Harry Leech was marooned in the heart of a furnace in a room without a door or window.

On most Saturdays Eugene Rabouille would leave his home near Beauvais about midnight and set snares for rabbits in the fields and woods. This Saturday night it was so wet and wretched that he was reluctant to drag himself away from his fireside. But at last he did so; after all, it would be Sunday next day, and he would not have to go to work at the button factory at Allonne; he could stay in bed all the morning if need be. Even so, the wet unfriendly woods seemed no place for a tired workman of fifty-seven, as he stepped out of his house and the gale almost tore the door from his hand.

He took a moment's shelter in the lee of a house to regain his breath, and looking up at the scudding clouds, he saw the dark shape of an airship over Beauvais, about a mile to the north. Even at that distance she looked enormous, a dark and gigantic cigar over the few faint lights of the town. The red and green navigation lamps glowed through the storm, and as she turned in the wind Rabouille could see the glow from the windows in the lounge and the passengers' quarters. None of this was any concern of his, and he had his snares to set, but all the same, after he had crossed the Meru road towards the plateau overlooking the town, he stopped again, looking up at R.101.

R.101 was over the Bois des Coutumes - not more than 150 feet up moving very slowly. The wind was forcing her towards the east.

'I clearly saw the passengers' quarters, well lit, and the green and red lights on the right and left of the airship,' he said later. 'Suddenly there was a violent squall. The airship dipped by the nose several times, and its fore part crashed into the north-west edge of the Bois des Coutumes. There was at once a tremendous explosion, which knocked me down.

'Soon flames rose into the sky to a great height - perhaps 300 feet. Everything was enveloped by them. I saw human figures running about like madmen in the wreck. Then I lost my head and ran away into the woods.'

As he ran he carried with him a fearful memory of the sight; the stern half of the airship sinking slowly as fire consumed it. Because he was two or three hundred yards away, the noise took time to travel, and he heard the engines running for a second or two after they had actually stopped. The sound pursued him as he plunged wildly through the wood, branches lacerating his face and tearing his clothes. Then he heard two explosions. These brought back the horror of what he had seen. He did not stop running until he reached home and barred the door against the memory. Then Eugene Rabouille, the man nearest to the airship as she crashed, crossed himself and went to bed.

M. Louis Petit, who kept the general store in Allonne village was also on his way to bed after a very busy night in his shop.

'Suddenly I heard a noise like a long roll of thunder,' he said. 'I ran out in the street, and quite low above the church opposite I saw something which looked like a lit-up village. I knew the "Zep" was due to pass over us, and I realized that something was wrong. The ship was moving broadside on. Suddenly all the lights in the airship went out, and a moment later they were all turned on again. Then again they went out, then on and out again. I remarked to my wife that each time the lights went on, the airship dropped a bit lower. Then with all the lights on, the airship nosedived. There was a mighty explosion - oh, something that you cannot imagine! It was as if the whole world had exploded.

'I telephoned to the police that the airship had crashed over the fields...'

Monsieur H Bard, of the Rue Cyprien Desgroux, Beauvais, was awakened by the Saint Etienne clock, just across the square from his house, striking two, and as he lay between sleep and waking, wondering why this very common sound should have so disturbed him, he heard engines in the air, and, like Rabouille, remembered that the British airship was due to pass over the town some time in the early hours.

He woke his wife and they opened their bedroom window. Peering through the rain they saw the R. 101 between 800 and 1,000 metres from the house, flying at a height of no more than 300 metres, and possibly less. The night was so bad and visibility was so poor that they only saw her as a dim, heavy shape. The noise of the engines came up clearly, as though she were running against the wind. They watched her disappear behind the top of the tower of Saint Etienne and then climbed back into bed.

M. Bard was already sinking into his interrupted sleep when his wife shook him.

"What's that light?' she asked.

Her husband opened his eyes and to his astonishment saw the whole sky glow with a growing intensity, so that their bedroom was lit up as though the dawn had come hours early. They looked at each other in amazement as from beyond the town came a rumble like distant thunder or great guns firing. The window panes shook and ratded in their frames. Then came a louder roar which made the house tremble and a great gust of wind that rattled all the panes. Then there was silence and darkness and the sound of rain on the roof.

Down in his hut in a clover field, a shepherd, Louis Tillier, of Bongenoult village, also heard the noise of the engines overhead, and, peering out, saw a stream of lights that reminded him of the lights of a passing train; only these were in the storm above his head. As he watched, the lights dipped, and there was a sudden roar and a huge flame swept up above the trees, lighting up the fields and the woods and the terrified eyes of his sheep.

Shortly before two o'clock Jules Edmond Patron, the secretary of Beauvais Police Station, also heard the engines, but instead of merely turning over in his sleep, he leapt out of bed, pulled on a pair of trousers and ran through the rain to the marketplace in the centre of the town. It was an historic moment, the passage of such a huge airship above his town, and where better to view it than from the heart of Beauvais? Above him he saw the dim shape of the airship and her glittering lights, then she was gone and he went back home. He had no time to undress again, though, for within minutes men were running through the streets beneath his window and beating on his door, shouting for aid. The airship he had just seen in the sky was down in the fields.

Binks peered out of the car towards the bows, 'Sky' Hunt's call, 'We're down, lads!' still in his ears. Instead of the glistening silver hull, he was looking at the naked frame of the airship glowing red-hot like the skeleton of some gigantic fish. Only scraps of burning fabric remained on the ribs; the rest had gone in a fury of flame that hissed and roared in the rain.

Bell peered out equally astonished at the nightmare view.

'We'd better get out of this, Joe,' he said, pulling in his head and mechanically turning off all the fuel oil taps.

Binks pulled his arm.

'No,' he said. 'Hang on.'

The wind was against them, blowing down the flames from the bow to the tail, and they could not hope to survive in that inferno. Their clothes and skin would be burnt off before they were half out of the car. The alternative of waiting was only slightly less grim, for sharing the engine car with them were metal drums containing 30 gallons of petrol to work the starting motor. Bell was, in fact, the senior of the two, and Binks realized that he should take orders from him, but as he said later, 'I knew I was right in staying.'

'Give way to me on this and we'll be all right,' he told Bell, for this was no time for argument. As they stood, flames began to lick up between the floorboards, scorching the soles of their feet. At best they had only a few moments before the petrol exploded; the only problem was, how to use that time to their advantage.

Then liquid of some kind came pouring down on them from above. Some streamed down Binks' face and into his mouth. He gave a cry of excitement.

'Water!' The ballast tanks had burst within the airship, and this accident undoubtedly saved their lives.

They both seized rags used for cleaning the engine, and held them up into the stream, and then threw them on the floor, treading out the flames.

Then, turning their backs to the wind they climbed out under the port quarter - the left-hand side of the stern - and jumped. They landed on all fours on the soft earth of a gentle slope.

'By going out with our backs to the fire we saved our eyesight,' says Binks now. 'We were burned on the face and hands, though, but didn't realize this until a bit later. The shock of the whole thing was so tremendous that even while we were staggering about, slithering in the mud, it all seemed more like a nightmare than reality. One moment we were in the greatest airship that had ever been made, as large and expensive as an ocean liner, and the next there was nothing but a mass of metal with a few of us shouting for help and trying to see whether anyone else was still alive.'

Painfully they crawled away from the glowing wreck, gasping for breath, for there seemed to be no air in all the night sky that they could breathe. In this they were quite right; there was none. In burning, the five and a half million cubic feet of hydrogen had used up a mass of surrounding oxygen, so that the survivors were like some ancient mariners of the sky, with air on every side, yet none that they could breathe.

As they crouched on the ground, gasping for breath, a third man came lumbering towards them, hands out as though warding off some fearful vision.

'Where are you? Is there anyone there?' he called, sensing them rather than seeing them.

'We're here, Binks and Bell. We're all right.'

The figure ran towards them, his face fearfully burned, his hair singed from his forehead, and in the glow from the still incandescent hull of the airship they recognized Harry Leech. He came nearer, and they saw that his hands and forearms were gashed and lacerated. These strong arms and his unusually powerful shoulders had undoubtedly saved his life, for when the lights went out and the door jammed in the smoking-room Harry Leech knew that unless he could force a way through the bulkhead to the outer air he would be sealed within an aerial tomb.

He picked up one of the tables by its legs and smashed it against the bulkhead. It disintegrated into a mass of useless, spongy fragments, for despite its solid appearance, carefully simulated to look like grained mahogany, it was only made of balsa wood without either weight or strength. Steadily and painfully he climbed up the steep incline of the floor and found another table, a chair, an ashtray, and smashed each in turn against the bulkhead. One after another they all disintegrated and he was left with a stump of wicker in his hand alone and helpless in the darkness. Insulated by alloy walls and hung in the heart of the vessel, he had no means of knowing what was happening outside, or if indeed the outside of the airship still existed. All he knew was that he was still alive and must either get out or die.

He began savagely kicking the metal bulkhead, raining blows on it with the sole of his foot, for like all the crew he was wearing canvas shoes in case of fire, and there was no strength in the toe. He paused a minute, listening, straining to hear any of the tell-tale sounds of creaking joints that would tell him that the structure of the airship was breaking up. He could hear nothing but the roar of blood in his ears. He wiped his hand across his face; it came away soaking with sweat.

If he couldn't kick his way out, then he would punch his way out. He groped his way along the sides of the bulkhead, until the smoothness of the metal gave way to the slightly rougher surface of asbestos which, though equally fireproof, would be much easier to get through. Presently he found it, and began to hammer it with his back, beating on it with his clenched fists, defying it to hold up against him.

At first it stayed firm, and then he seized a catch that had been loosened from the wall and tore it away. Then he widened a jagged hole through the thin metal bulkhead, and the thick smoky smell of burning fuel oil, sweetened with the sickly stench of other burning came up strongly, making his eyes run, almost overpowering him. He kept on tearing at the small hole, widening it, until it was large enough for him to climb through, and then he was out in one of the companionways. Instead of smooth walls, handrails and painted canvas roof, only naked girders and struts remained. And everywhere was flame, yellow, orange and terrible. He had escaped from the frying pan literally into the fire.

As he stared about him he saw a gap ahead in the side of the airship, and without thinking - because there was no time to think and no other decision to reach even if there had been time - he jumped. Years afterwards, Harry Leech still remembered that moment of falling as if it had happened but a few days before.

'I didn't know what was happening. I only knew that I had to get out of the airship while there was time. I was lucky, for when I jumped I landed in a tree, and the branches cushioned my fall. It had been pouring with rain, and as the branches shook when I landed in them, they seemed to empty their rain on me. It was the best drink of my life. I had been well and truly cooked. That rain cooled me off.'

Down in the meadow the three men found their voices. Already villages were running with lanterns and torches, and now that the roar of the hydrogen fire had died they could hear voices shouting directions to each other. In Beauvais, local gendarmes on horseback and on foot were rousing householders and demanding sheets or any other linen to use as bandages for the living or winding sheets for the dead.

Binks, Leech and Bell, forgetting their own injuries - for the intensity of the shock had numbed them, and it was only some time afterwards that they felt the pain from their terrible burns - went up along the port side of the airship to see if they could find anyone alive. The wind was blowing the fire and the storm towards them, so that their eyes smarted and they gasped for breath, choking in the black oil smoke. The heat was tremendous, and the great alloy girders hissed in the streaming rain. The scene was lit as bright as day for a wide area around, and on the edge of darkness the lights and torches of the rescuers from the village danced like gadflies. The three survivors found one man who had been flung clear and, though clearly near the point of death, was still conscious and able to recognize them.

As they knelt beside him he indicated that he wanted them to remove his jacket. As carefully as they could, trembling with reaction, sodden with rain on one side, and almost scorched by the heat of the flames on the other, they pulled it off, and his lips began to move. Even in the glow of the airship his cheeks were grey and lifeless.

Take it home for me, please. Take it home,' he whispered, and the sound of his own voice seemed to rally him. 'I've got some Players' in there,' he went on, and nodded towards one of the pockets in his coat. They rummaged in it and pulled out a flat tin of fifty. Each took one gratefully, and then discovered that they had not a match between them. For a moment they looked at each other, and then they all had the same thought at once. Binks took his cigarette out of his mouth, walked a couple of paces towards a piece of glowing wreckage, and lit it from the red-hot metal. That light was the most expensive he ever used; it had cost more than a million pounds.

As they crouched by the side of the dying man, another man came running towards them shouting in English. He was George Darling, grandson of the famous trainer, who lived in France. He and a friend, Marcel Depaubuis, a musician of renown, had planned a morning's shooting and were already up early and dressing when they saw the airship flying overhead.

'It was a wonderful sight,' said Darling afterwards, but within a few seconds there was what he described as 'a burst of thunder and lightning - a moment of nothing - and then flames that seemed to reach the sky.'

He pulled a jacket on over his pyjamas, stuck his feet into top boots and raced with his friend to his car. Within minutes they reached the beetroot field where the airship had made her last landing.

The first thing I saw,' he said later, 'were three figures - three men struggling about like gnomes who had leapt out of the fiery furnace behind them.'

Leech grabbed a piece of burning wreckage to use as a torch. 'Come and help,' he called as Darling ran up. 'My pals are burning to death.' He dashed back towards the airship.

By now others were also arriving with poles and sticks, and hammers and axes, and they went into the control car smashing their way through the doors that fire had sealed. Despite their frantic search for survivors only three others lived to remember this fearful morning in the rain.

One was A J Cook, the engineer in the aft port car, who took over at two o'clock from his comrade, Robert Blake, checked the instruments, and then settled down to what he expected to be a routine watch.

Five minutes later the ship took a steep dive and the engine telegraph rang to 'slow'.

He tried to squeeze out of the doorway of the car towards the ship, he explained afterwards, but it was one mass of flames. The heat was terrific, so he turned back to the port side of the car. A girder had fallen across the entrance and he seemed to be hopelessly trapped. He lay down on the top of an oil tank for a moment, and then, in a desperate effort, leapt up, put his hand out and managed to push the girder to one side with the back of his hand.

'I then jumped over the side of the car and found that I had landed on some grass among trees. I made my way through the wood, where I saw a gas valve lying on the ground, and then I came to an open space. Looking round I saw sparks trailing me and I found that the overalls I was wearing were smouldering. My hands were hurting terribly. The fear of being burned again must have made me pull off my flying boots and overalls. I put my boots back on again and threw the overalls away.'

Arthur Disley, the second survivor, was in charge of the airship's electrical gear which he had inspected twice during the night; the first time just after the airship left the mooring mast at Cardington, and again at about nine forty-five, because one of the big switches had 'tripped' and thrown the whole airship into darkness and some confusion.

He had just gone to sleep in his bunk when the airship dipped over Beauvais and then began to climb. The next thing he heard was 'Sky' Hunt's cry: 'We're down, lads', and the Coxswain ran past to warn the crew of approaching calamity.

As the airship hit the ground, the lights went off, and, acting on instinct, Disley pressed the button that cut out the dynamos to try to minimize the risk of short circuits and fire. Miraculously, he was still alive, and at once he set out across the sticky sodden fields towards the town to seek a telephone. Then, while confusion reigned around him, he impressed upon the local French operator the urgency of the situation and within minutes was speaking to the Air Ministry in London and giving them the first official news of the disaster.

Victor Savory, the only other survivor who lived more than a few hours, was in the starboard midship engine car, when the airship dipped and flung him against the starting engine. The big diesel engine was running at cruising speed, 825 revolutions a minute, and even as the airship ploughed into the ground, he noticed, surprised, dazed, almost stunned, that the engine was still running normally, and as though nothing at all had happened. Flames surrounded him, scorching, dazing, choking him with the thick oil fumes, but somehow, with his hands in front of him, he staggered out until he felt the rain on his face and knew that he was free.

At 3 o'clock that Sunday morning, the telephone rang by Ralph Booth's bed. He reached out for it sleepily. Squadron Leader Sydney Nixon, who was temporarily commanding the Royal Airship Works at Cardington, was on the line.

'We've got some bad news,' he said, his voice sounding thin and excited over the wire. 'R.101 has made a crash landing in France. You'd better come along immediately to the station.'

'I don't believe it,' Booth answered. They said the same thing about us when we were flying over the Atlantic. It's just one of those stories.'

'Well, anyhow, come along. This sounds serious.'

Booth got out of bed, dressed, and drove over to the station in his Talbot car. A light was burning in Nixon's office, and his face was grave as the two men met.

'It must be true,' he said. 'Disley has telephoned through to the Air Ministry giving their position and the names of one or two survivors'

Booth stayed in the little office with Nixon, until the dawn came up over the wide airfield, still trampled and muddy with the feet of the spectators who had watched the airship set out less than twelve hours before. The telephone did not ring again; there was no more news.

About six o'clock, when there seemed no point in staying further, for there was nothing more anyone could do, he went home and told his wife what had happened.

'We must go and tell Olive,' she said at once. He nodded; this was something that had to be faced, and together they set off in their car. The morning was fresh and sunny, and the countryside had a well-washed look; he thought ironically that, compared with the terrible storm of the night, this was ideal airship weather.

The Irwins had been living in a large and modern bungalow, set back from the road outside Bedford. The Booths stopped some way from the entrance and walked along the lane and up the short drive in the hope that they would not disturb Mrs Irwin. They knew that her sister and brother-in-law were staying with her, sleeping in one of the side bedrooms, so they tiptoed up to the window, which was open, and called to them softly. But they were both heavy sleepers, and even when they had awoken they could not grasp why the Booths were calling on them at such an early hour.

'Come round to the front door,' whispered Mrs Booth. 'We want your help. We've got some bad news.'

They began to climb out of bed, and the Booths went round to the front of the house to wait for them. When they came in sight of the front porch, however, they saw a figure already standing there, wrapped in a dressing gown: Mrs Irwin, with her face as white as her husband's had been when the O'Neills saw him on board the airship a few days previously.

'It's all right,' she said quietly, turning to them. 'You needn't worry. I know. You see, Bird is Irish and I'm Scottish. We both knew he wasn't coming back again. There's nothing more to be said.'

Slowly she turned on her heel and went back into the house.

1. From the introduction by I Ramsay MacDonald to Lord Thomson's novel *Smaranda*.

CHAPTER SEVEN

The Real Memorial

By the time the Booths returned home, their telephone was already ringing. The Air Ministry wanted Booth to fly that morning to Beauvais for an examination of the wreckage with other airship experts, and to interview any survivors who were well enough to give an account of the airship's last moments. One of those in the party was Mr McWade, the resident inspector at Cardington of the Airworthiness Inspection Department, whose report on the unairworthiness of R. 101 had never reached the Secretary of the Air Ministry. They flew on the normal London-Paris flight of Imperial Airways, but the aeroplane was diverted for them and landed at Beauvais.

Even in death the R. 101 was impressive. From a quarter of a mile away her great frame of girders towered above the trees, and at the tip of the enormous tail fin the Royal Air Force ensign still flew, the only piece of fabric the fire had spared.

It was difficult to believe that this smoke-blackened skeleton, like the bones of some giant fish, was actually the frame of the airship that had left Cardington only the previous day, and not the girders for some great new building among the trees. As the aeroplane circled before landing, the silent group of experts were comforted in the midst of tragedy by this proof that at least their calculations of stress and strain had been proved accurate by the fiercest test of all. The crash was not due to faulty construction or to bad design.

All the gasbags and the outer fabric had been completely burned away, but still the gasbag harnesses remained, a fine and elaborate tracing of thin wires looking in the afternoon light as though giant spiders had been weaving some strange web in the midst of the ruined vessel. Towards the centre of the airship such fittings as water tanks, the great gas valves, even parts of a staircase, were plainly recognizable. A row of gilded pillars, the last remnants of the lounge, glittered grotesquely.

The nose of the airship ran into a thin wood of hazel and oak trees, and the tail, as large as the latticed entrance of Paddington Station, lay out in an open field. The giant rudder rocked slowly to and fro in the afternoon breeze. The oil that experts had said could never burn had soaked into the earth all round and then the sodden ground had blazed like a wick, roaring in a fearful frying pan of heat and light, in the midst of which villagers and local firemen had staggered, searching for survivors and dragging body after body out from the blaze. As the experts arrived on the scene, flames were still licking parts of the airship and burning the trodden earth.

The bodies had been carried a little way into the wood of stunted trees and laid out in a row under sheets willingly provided by local people. Some peasants had placed posies of flowers near them, and others, mostly old women with black shawls over their heads, had brought candles and knelt in prayer until daylight in the churned mud by the blackened shell of the airship. The survivors were already being cared for by nuns in the local hospital with every kindness, but conditions were a little primitive; this particular hospital had been built by Napoleon as a barracks, and was rather lacking in modern amenities. As soon as the survivors were fit to be moved, arrangements were made for them to be flown back to England for further treatment.

The concert room of the town hall had been converted into a mortuary, and so that no one's susceptibilities should be offended, all religious emblems were forbidden. The walls had been draped with black cloth. The potted palms that had graced the stage for concerts were stacked to the ceiling at one end; at the other hung the tricolour of France, and each coffin, resting on trestles, was covered by a small Union Jack.

Throughout Monday, French army lorries and carts drove from the wreckage to the town, three miles away, carrying the new coffins. Crowds had gathered from miles around, so that by midday the lorries were driving through lanes of silent watchers, many of whom made the sign of the cross as the coffins passed by. Never had so many people collected in Beauvais; it was the centre of the world's attention. The French Cabinet ordered a day of mourning in France and throughout the colonies. As the coffins were carried into the town hall - called, for the time being, The Chapel of Repose for the Sons of Britain' - a sudden storm started unexpectedly in the warm morning, with a flash of lightning and the rattle of hailstones on the cobbles round the lorries.

Most of the dead were unidentifiable. Each of the coffins was numbered, however, and the same number was also on a small box in which were placed any articles retrieved from the body -a steel pencil, a cigarette case, the shell of a watch - that had survived the fire. Afterwards, attempts were made to identify these sad relics.

The feeling of immense tragedy that silenced the crowds at Beauvais was shared by the rest of the world. King George V, who only a few weeks before had watched the great airship drone over Sandringham, sent a message of condolence to the Prime Minister: 'I am horrified to hear of this national disaster.'

Ramsay MacDonald announced that he was 'grieved beyond words at the loss of so many splendid men, whose sacrifice has been added to that glorious list of Englishmen who, on uncharted seas and unexplored lands, have gone into the unknown as pioneers and pathfinders, and have met death...'

The Kings of Belgium, Denmark, Egypt, Italy, Sweden, Norway, the ex-King of Portugal, and the Regent of Hungary all sent messages of sympathy. So did Mussolini, and the Presidents of France, Switzerland, Lithuania and Portugal. The American Secretary of State and the Governors-General and Prime Ministers of the Dominions also expressed deep regret, and thousands of letters and telegrams came from lesser people who had wished a safe journey for the R.101's crew. John Masefield, the Poet Laureate, wrote: The sudden loss of so many of our best must touch every feeling heart with the thought that these men died while advancing man's mastery over the elements, increasing his knowledge, and breaking down his boundaries. The men of this race have ever been pioneers, content to spend themselves thus. May a sense of the immortality of all high endeavour comfort those grieving for them.'

If in life the designers and crew had been rushed, in death their fame was international, and now that time had no meaning for them, it was ironic that nothing was to be hurried or too good for their memory.

In Shortstown, Royal Air Force dispatch riders delivered notes to the next of kin of all the crew, and after them came the reporters; it is hard to say which were the more unwelcome. Other people, doubtless meaning well, arrived in cars at the little houses in Shortstown and invited themselves inside to console the widows and their families. Not all had kindly motives. One widow discovered, after the initial flood of callers, most of whom she had never seen before, that not only was her husband's gold watch missing, but also his set of tools - and even his bicycle. She was not the only widow to discover, too late, that some people came with condolences and left with more than they brought.

Meanwhile, news reached Shortstown that Rigger Samuel Church, who just before the crash had been sent to the front of the airship to release some water ballast by hand in a last desperate attempt to bring up her bows (because all the other ballast had been shed at the mast in Cardington as she set off) was seriously injured and not expected to live. At once his father and fiancee set off together for Beauvais. First they drove to Henlow airfield in the hope of chartering an aeroplane, but a gale was blowing too strongly for the plane to take off. There was no sign that it would abate, so they travelled by train and boat to Calais and then drove to Beauvais. They arrived shortly after seven in the evening after a most harassing journey, but all in vain. Church had died before they reached his bedside.

In Bedford, on the Sunday and throughout the following week, blinds were drawn in nearly every house, and the Salvation Army band marched through the streets playing the Dead March from *Saul* over and over again. Everyone wanted news, for almost everyone was concerned, but only the *Sunday Express* had printed the news that Sunday morning. This was due to the initiative of the night executive on duty, Arthur Christiansen, a young man from Wallasey, who on his own authority stopped the presses in the early morning, roused out his staff from their beds, and completely 'remade' the front page - a prodigious feat of journalism for which he was very soon rewarded by being made editor of the *Daily Express* - a position he was to hold with brilliance and distinction for many years.

Not every house in Shortstown and Bedford had wireless sets to receive the broadcast news, and by evening, after a day of fearful rumours, crowds besieged the offices in the High Street for copies of the *Bedford and District Circular,* a local paper printed every Sunday. Police formed them into a queue and then someone started the cry that they should go instead to the printing works in Howard Street, and so hundreds rushed there and papers were sold as fast as they left the machines. The demand for copies went on long after the presses stopped at ten o'clock that night.

All Monday and until Tuesday morning the coffins lay in state in Beauvais Town Hall, guarded by soldiers, gendarmes and four Red Cross nurses. On the Tuesday they were moved to Boulogne, and a great procession, with full service honours, mustered in the main square of Beauvais. More than a hundred thousand people gathered to watch them go. Two battalions of the French 51st Infantry Regiment in their pale-blue uniforms, with steel helmets and polished bayonets, faced the Town Hall, with two mounted squadrons of Spahi Cavalry in their magnificent robes. There was a detachment from the French naval airship base at Orly, and in places of honour stood the three R. 101 survivors who were well enough to attend: Joe Binks, Arthur Bell and Harry Leech, all still wearing the clothes they had on when the airship crashed.

A hundred and one guns fired the salute shortly before eleven o'clock, bands played 'God Save The King' and the 'Marseillaise', and then the long line of twenty-three army carts, each drawn by four horses, and each containing two coffins set off for the station. They headed a procession of Beauvais firemen who had gallantly tried to fight the fire, with long columns of infantry, gendarmes, marines, ex-Service associations, nuns and Girl Guides. Overhead, Nieuport-Delage fighters and Breguet XIX reconnaissance aeroplanes flew in formation. Beauvais station had been decorated with hundreds of Union Jacks and French flags hung with crape. At Boulogne, where the train was unloaded, the coffins were carried aboard two British destroyers, HMS *Tempest* and HMS *Tribune*. Thousands had lined the railway line through northern France, and at Etaples, the largest British war cemetery in France, the Union Jack flew at half mast.

The tide was low, and the tips of the destroyers' funnels were level with the side of the quay. As the doors of the railway vans opened massed bands again played first the 'Marseillaise' and then 'God Save the King'. Squads of firemen toiled back and forth with the coffins, which were swung by a crane aboard the nearer destroyer. Even then things were not going perfectly for the men of the ill-fated airship. One destroyer had developed propeller trouble on the crossing from England, and at the last moment, in case she broke down, it was decided that all the coffins were to be carried in one ship instead of two.

Wreaths and bunches of flowers were heaped on the coffins, and sailors stood round them with heads bowed and arms reversed. As the last order was given rain began to fall, and with searchlights playing ceaselessly on the flags and the flowers, the ships drew slowly out into the darkness.

From Dover searchlights reached out to meet them while they were still at sea, and a special train bore the coffins to Victoria, still under Union Jacks and in newly-painted vans lit by dim blue bulbs. Even the engine carried a wreath.

They arrived at Victoria on the stroke of midnight, and the entire station had been cleared for the occasion. A small party waited to unload the coffins on to Service trucks and take them first to a mortuary and then, for a further lying-in-state, to Westminster Hall. All officers who had travelled back to England with them had been cautioned not to speak to anyone at Victoria lest the inquirer should be connected with the Press, for much service indignation had been aroused by a British newspaper report of certain statements which an officer was alleged to have made about fragments of wreckage found some distance away from the scene of the disaster. This was officially denied, but the denial did not alter the fact that some wreckage *had* been found miles from the crash - possibly blown there by the force of the explosion.

After lying in state at Westminster Hall, there was a Memorial Service at St Paul's, where the King was represented by the Prince of Wales. Representatives of every foreign power with an embassy or legation in Britain were also present. At the same time a requiem mass was said at Westminster Cathedral for the four Roman Catholics who had died in the disaster. The officiating priest was Father Harry Rope, brother of Squadron Leader Rope.

Then on the Saturday, exactly a week after the airship had set out, the bodies of the passengers and crew were brought back to Cardington to demonstrations of national grief that had previously only been associated with the deaths of Kings. More than half a million people turned out to watch the funeral procession from Westminster Hall to Euston Station. It was two miles long and took an hour to pass. During the afternoon there was a two minutes' silence at Brooklands in the middle of a meeting of the British Motor-Cycle Racing Club. All clubs affiliated to the Football Association observed a similar silence, the teams standing drawn up on the field; and even the bookmakers and racegoers at Kempton Park stood bareheaded for two minutes' tribute.

Immediately the funeral procession had passed along Whitehall, scores of young men hurried into the Air Ministry to enlist for the Air Force. The RAF reported that since the disaster its recruiting department had been working at full pressure and waiting lists were longer than had ever been known before.

At Euston the crowd was the biggest ever remembered. Over the last half-mile of the route only the people who had arrived very early in the morning had any chance of seeing the procession at all. Thousands who later poured out of the Underground at Euston were diverted into back streets behind the station and so saw nothing whatever, so dense were the throngs between them and the cortege. The vast whispering throng spread to the station roof, the tops of buildings and to every balcony within sight.

So many wreaths arrived that there was no room for them all on the coffins and they had to be loaded onto other RAF tenders. Their scent filled the autumn air with a cloying sweetness. Two engines, the 'Arabic' and the 'Persia', drew the train, the former bearing a huge wreath of red, white and blue flowers under a glass case, the gift of the London, Midland and Scottish Railway.

Windows overlooking the railway lines were packed with people; platelayers on the line and the drivers of other locomotives stopped work and removed their hats as the funeral train passed by. Even in the suburbs the crowds were out; at Willesden hundreds stood in the road overlooking the railway, and there were silent crowds at every station on the way. Saturday afternoon gardeners ceased digging their allotments; motorists stopped their cars and stood beside them at attention; flags flew at half mast on church towers, and from poles rigged up in the back gardens of small houses all along the route.

Finally, at a quarter to two, the train steamed into Bedford station, where waiting bearers walked up to the carriages, and in a deep silence lifted down the first coffin. At that precise moment the quiet was dramatically broken as two flights of bombers flew overhead in spearhead formation.

An RAF firing party with reversed arms led the procession to Cardington; then came the grey lorries with pipe-clayed tyres, each lorry laden with two coffins, still with their Union Jacks half hidden under the flowers. Of the forty-eight coffins only fourteen bore the names of the dead on aluminium plates. On all the rest the inscription was simply: To the memory of the unknown airman who died on October 5.' The plates had been made from metal used in the airship.

Bedford observed a day of mourning; all shops were shuttered and there was no traffic on the streets. Blinds were drawn in the houses as the crowd of thousands poured out all morning towards Cardington, and then massed on the path overlooking the station. Most were wearing black, and many carried flowers. At Cardington the police threw a cordon round the village, and allowed no wheeled traffic to enter.

In the churchyard labourers had worked all night by the light of flares to dig the enormous grave for the burial, tidying the sandy soil where it sloped into the grave and covering it with bronze and white chrysanthemums and fresh green turf which also lined the bottom of the grave. A boarded ramp led down from the top, ready for the coffins.

So great were the crowds here that by early afternoon 500 police and special constables, with 100 ambulance men, lined the streets; so long was the funeral procession that when the last tender was on the outskirts of Bedford, the head was halfway to the churchyard. The sound of the escorting aeroplanes, and the howling of a dog, were the only things to break the silence, save for the tolling of the church bell, which was rung for half an hour before the procession arrived.

It was nearly four o'clock when the Air Force lorries appeared in the early October dusk and the service began. The Anglican Bishop of St Albans, tall in his silk gown and crimson hood, with the Roman Catholic Bishop, robed in crimson and attended by his acolytes carrying incense, conducted the service, with the Vicar of Cardington, the Rev Sydney Seccombe, the Senior Chaplain of the RAF with two staff chaplains, and two nonconformist ministers. The band played 'Abide with Me', as the coffins were slowly brought in, one by one, from the road, and carried down the slope to the T-shaped grave, where they were laid in rows, still covered with their flags.

It took half an hour to lay out all the dead from R. 101 in their common grave among the flowers. As the Vicar intoned the first sentences of the burial service, 'I am the Resurrection and the Life... The Lord gave, and the Lord hath taken away. Blessed be the name of the Lord... Yea, though I walk through the valley of the shadow of death, I will fear no evil, for thou art with me...', the only sound was the crunch of boots on the ground as the bearers bore in coffin after coffin.

The Chaplain read the lesson and the Bishop of St Albans took the main part of the service, while the aircraft in the darkening sky flew and dipped in salute. Then came the Last Post and Reveille from the trumpeters, and a peal of muffled bells. Slowly the crowds began to drift away, and the deepening dusk shrouded the outline of the two great airship sheds and the mooring mast.

On the Tuesday after the disaster Mr Harry Price, an inquirer into psychic phenomena, held a seance at the modest building in London which he called The National Laboratory of Psychical Research'. With Mrs Eileen Garrett acting as medium he hoped to establish contact with the spirit of Sir Arthur Conan Doyle, who had died in July, leaving instructions in his will that such attempts should be made. But in the darkened room, when Mrs Garrett's voice changed and she began to speak deeply, she did not have a message from the author. Instead she spelt out IRVING or IRWIN. People sat forward in their chairs, immediately recognizing the name. Again the tone of the medium's voice changed, so that a man appeared to be speaking. He announced himself as 'Flight-Lieutenant H Carmichael Irwin', who had been captain of the airship R.101. As he spoke, in short staccato sentences, his voice rose and fell, tailing away almost to a whisper, as though he were speaking under great stress and difficulty.

'The whole bulk of the dirigible was entirely and absolutely too much for her engines' capacity,' said the voice. 'Engines too heavy. Useful lift too small. Oil pipe plugged.'

As he went on the voice gained depth and authority, and the words came tumbling out in a cascade that horrified the hearers.

'...Flying too low altitude and could never rise. Disposable lift could not be utilized. Load too great for long flight... Cruising speed bad and ship badly swinging. Severe tension on the fabric which is chafing... Engines wrong - too heavy -cannot rise. Never reached cruising altitude - same in trials. Too short trials. No one knew the ship properly. Weather bad for long flight. Fabric all waterlogged and ship's nose is down. Impossible to rise. Cannot trim.

'Almost scraped the roofs at Achy. Kept to railway. At inquiry to be held later it will be found that the superstructure of the envelope contained no resilience and had far too much weight in envelope. The added middle section was entirely wrong...too heavy, too much over-weighted for the capacity of engines...'

Neither Mr Price nor Mrs Garrett had any technical knowledge of airships, or indeed of anything aeronautical, but the comments which had issued through the mouth of Mrs Garrett appear to have been technically correct.

The engines *were* heavier than had been expected; the airship *was* sluggish to handle and slow to rise. Further, the oil pressure *had* caused concern when R.101 was over the Channel, a fact then known only to the survivors, for it had not been included in any radio messages sent from air to land, and did not become public knowledge until after the Inquiry. Achy, where the voice said R. 101 nearly scraped the roofs, is a small village north of Beauvais on the airship's line of flight, and although not on all ordinary tourists' maps, it was marked on the large-scale maps which the airship carried.

Harry Price was so disturbed by this communication that he sent one copy of the statement to Sir John (later Lord) Simon, Chairman of the Court of Inquiry which had been ordered to discover, if possible, the causes of the disaster, and another to the Air Ministry.'

On 1 April 1931, the Court of Inquiry issued its Report. Sir John Simon, who had sat with Colonel J T C Moore-Brabazon and Professor C E Inglis as assessors, decided that the immediate cause of the disaster was a sudden loss of gas in a forward gasbag at a time when the nose of the airship was being depressed by a downward current of air. Other factors, such as the fact that the watch had changed at two and the new men had not had time to get the 'feel' of the ship, probably contributed. The Report of the Inquiry added: 'In the construction of R.101 the designers broke away almost completely from conventional methods. Originality and courage in design are not to be deprecated, but there is an obvious danger in giving too many separate hostages to fortune at one time... During the construction, and in the early flights of the R.101, this policy of cautious experiment at each step was admirably fulfilled; but in the later stages, when it became important to avoid further postponement and the flight to India thus became urgent, there was a tendency to rely on limited experiment instead of tests under all conditions...and the R.101 started for India before she could be regarded as having emerged successfully from all the exhaustive tests proper to an experimental stage...

'It is clear that if those responsible had been entirely free to choose the time and the weather in which the R.101 should start for the first flight ever undertaken by any airship to India, and if the only considerations governing their choice were considerations of meteorology and of preparation for the voyage, the R.101 would not have started when she did. She was undertaking a novel task in weather conditions worse than any to which she had ever been exposed in flight, and with the prospect of more unfavourable weather after she started. She had never gone through trials which proved by their length and conditions that she was well able to cope with a continuance of unfavourable circumstances. The programme of trials drawn up by her Captain has never been carried through, and the intended length of her last trial was avowedly cut down in order to provide a litde more time for preparation before the date which was contemplated for her to start for India. No adequate speed trials had ever been carried through, and indeed this fact was so clearly recognized that an official of the Air Ministry urged that she should conduct such speed trials on her voyage to India.

'It is impossible to avoid the conclusion that the R.101 would not have started for India on the evening of October 4 if it had not been that reasons of public policy were considered as making it highly desirable for her to do so if she could...'

After the first grief passed, a great reaction against airships set in. The R. 100, which had cost £450,000, was confined to her shed for a year and then broken up with axes, and the pieces crushed by steamroller so that they could be sold for scrap.

R.101 was broken up in Beauvais by the Sheffield firm of Thos. W Ward Ltd, and the pieces brought home to be made into pots and pans.

The masts in Montreal and Ismailia were dismantled. The problem at Karachi, where Commander Watt and his 'gassing and mooring party' still remained after the disaster, was more complicated, since the fate of the huge airship shed there had also to be decided, and it seemed too large to demolish easily. Eventually the mast was sold to the local railway company and dismantled so that the steel could be used for building bridges. Various plans were proposed for demolishing the shed, which had cost thousands to build. Most of them entailed blowing it up, but there were other buildings nearby, so this was impossible. So vast was the shed, and so great the deterioration under the conditions of sun and monsoon that Watt had a band of eighteen men painting it continually. As they finished one coat, so it was time to start again with another. This went on, with no decision taken, until the war, when Americans arriving in India for the China-Burma-India theatre of operations used it as a transit camp. As many as 3,000 men slept in the shed at a time, and still had room to spare.

At Cardington, the great sheds built to house R.100 and R. 101 still stand. (*Information correct at time of writing*) During the war barrage balloons were made and stored there.

So much for the materials: what of the people involved?

Wing Commander Booth, who successfully flew R.100 to Canada and back, lives in retirement in Dorset. Arthur Bell and Joe Binks are still at Cardington on Service work. For years afterwards, Binks would wake up at two o'clock in the morning, the hour when the airship began to fall. Harry Leech, who was awarded the Albert Medal in recognition of his bravery in re-entering the burning wreckage to rescue a comrade, left England in December 1930 to help Kaye Don with attempts on the land speed record in America. He has also worked on record attempts with Sir Malcolm Campbell and his son Donald Campbell. During the war he was with Nevil Shute testing and developing mechanical inventions. He is retired, but his work is his life, and he spends a great deal of time developing a machine to hold radium seeds, needed in the search for a cure for cancer, and still looks back with affection on his days with the airships. 'One thing that R.101 proved,' he says, 'is that politics and experimental work don't mix.'

Arthur Disley, who received the Order of the British Empire for telephoning details of the disaster to the Air Ministry from Beauvais, is still with the Ministry of Civil Aviation. Some time ago he was asked whether he would fly again in airships. 'I'd go if I had to,' he replied. 'But I wouldn't rush.' In 1933 an impressive memorial was unveiled to the dead at Beauvais, and in 1955, on the anniversary of the disaster, a further service was held there to show that the forty-eight men are still remembered.

Something of the dour courage and determination that characterized all the airship men belonged also to their widows, only three of whom remarried. Most made new lives for themselves and their families by their own efforts, for although an R.101 Fund was launched, it came at a time of national depression, and only £1,500 was raised. Much of this went on paying for their memorial at

Cardington, and when the Fund was finally wound up in the autumn of 1956 the twenty-nine widows who could be traced received £19 9s. 9d. each. After this final payout, a small dividend arrived unexpectedly, and this was used to buy an inscribed vase to place near the memorial in Cardington Church.

Mrs Richmond says that Colonel Richmond's last words to her on that Saturday afternoon at Cardington a generation ago - 'Keep the flag flying' - have often cheered her.

'We always remember them now when things go wrong,' she says. Her husband is also remembered by a screen to his memory in Highams Park Church, and a bed in the local hospital.

Mrs Gent found herself with a pension of £97 a year and an annual allowance of another £16 for the education of her son, and so took a job supervising staff at the Institute of Medical Psychology to eke this out. The effort was worthwhile, for her son Laurence inherited his father's scientific ability, and won a scholarship from Bedford Modern School to King's College; there he won two more research scholarships. He is now a doctor of philosophy and science.

Mrs Rope built a chapel in memory of her husband at Kesgrave, off the Ipswich-Woodbridge road. Her son, Crispin, who was born after his father's death, laid the foundation stone in June 1931, when he was only eight months old. A scale model of the R. 101 hangs in the chancel arch, and certain door fittings are made of metal salvaged from the airship.

Mrs Johnston died shortly after the disaster, and her son grew up under the care of an old friend, now Sir Frederick Tymms. It was Johnston's wish that the boy should become an Air Force officer, and that wish has been realized; he is a Wing Commander.

Johnston is still remembered, as the organizer of the Guild of Air Pilots and Navigators, which now has more than a thousand members and was granted Livery by the City in 1956. He pioneered this Guild to uphold the dignity and status of professional pilots and navigators, and it does this magnificently. The Duke of Edinburgh is Grand Master, an honour Sir Sefton Brancker was the first to hold.

Brancker's son - one of the first trainees in Imperial Airways, and who actually heard the news of the crash at Ismailia where he had hoped to welcome his father - is also in aviation. At the time of writing he is a senior executive with the International Air Transport Association, based in Montreal.

Although the loss of R. 101 and so many brilliant men ended airship experiments in Britain, much had already been learned that was of incalculable value to air travel in the years that followed.

Writing in the centenary number of *The Engineer,* Sir Harold Roxbee Cox, who had been closely associated with the design of R.101, said: 'It is, to some of us who worked for several years on the design and construction of the last British airships R. 100 and R.101, a consolation to remember that whilst the object of our endeavour, an all-red airship route across the world, was never achieved, and although the great airships are no more than great sad ghosts, yet the advances made in structural design and computation as a result of the endeavour have had an influence on the development of structures which has been wholly beneficial...'

Of equal importance have been the great advances made in the field of aerial meteorology, which started in the airship age and has now been brought to a fine pitch of achievement in the days of the jet.

With the end of airships as passenger-carrying projects in Britain, work turned with renewed intensity to developing the aeroplane, and the energies and enthusiasms which had consumed and sustained those who worked on the ships of the sky were now brought to bear on faster, more manoeuvrable machines. Here again lessons learned at such cost in the airship R. 101 had their meaning, for much had been discovered about the light metals such as duralumin and stainless steel that was of particular importance at a time when aeroplane construction was changing from wood to metal in order to cope with the much higher speeds involved. Indeed, it was as well this interest in aeroplanes quickened when it did, for the Battle of Britain was won barely ten years after the last flight of R.101.

Thus the abiding memorial to those who made that final journey is not to be found in Cardington or Beauvais, magnificent as these monuments to them may be. Their best memorial lies in the achievements they initiated. It is written anew in vapour trails above the clouds every time an airliner spans a storm to complete a flight on schedule with an ease we take for granted, but for which they died.

1. For fuller details see Appendix.

APPENDIX

Just over three weeks after the strange seance referred to in the last chappter, Major Oliver Villiers, who had driven his friend and colleague Sir Sefton Brancker to Cardington on that Saturday to board the airship, had a friend staying with him who was interested in spiritualism. The Major himself did not claim any powers of clairvoyance, but he sometimes became aware of the presence of any great friend who had 'passed over', and one evening, alone after the rest of the household had gone to bed, he was musing on the fact that he had lost such good friends as Brancker, Scott, Irwin, Johnston and Colmore, when he suddenly felt that Irwin was very near. It was as though Major Villiers heard Irwin say: 'For God's sake let me talk to you, it's all ghastly; I must speak to you.'

In his thoughts Major Villiers promised he would do all in his power to get into communication with him, and at that Irwin's presence seemed to go from the room. Villiers fully intended to carry out his promise but he did not know any reliable medium. Next morning he told his friend that someone who had recently died was in great distress and had implored him to make contact. His friend advised him to consult Mrs Garrett, who, although on the point of leaving for America, delayed her departure to see him. Through her services Major Villiers had seven long talks with a voice which he was convinced was Irwin's, and also with other voices which he was sure belonged to his friends who had gone down with the R. 101.

The first seance took place at 7 pm on 31 October 1930. For the first half-hour various individuals made their presence known to the control spirit, but nobody Major Viliers knew or in whom he had any interest. The seance looked like being a failure, but then, after a pause, a faint voice was heard saying: 'Irwin, Irwin. Don't go, please.' Villiers was convinced that this was the voice of Flight-Lieutenant Irwin, and at this seance - and at the subsequent meetings - a verbatim transcript was taken, and two copies were made. Major Villiers sent one to Sir John Simon, and has made the only other copy available for this book. From it the following extracts have been taken.

On the first occasion Major Villiers heard as described above, what he believed was Irwin's voice. Irwin seemed distressed. His first words were, 'We feel like damned murderers. It's awful, old man - awful! We ought to have said No!'

He went on: 'She was too heavy by several tons... During the afternoon before starting I noticed that the gas indicator was going up and down, which showed there was a leakage or escape which I could not stop or rectify at the time, around the valves. The goldbeater gas skins are not strong enough, and the constant movement of the gasbags acting like bellows, is constantly causing internal pressure of the gas, which causes a leakage of valves... I knew we were almost doomed.

Then, later on, the meteorological charts came in, and Scottie [Major Scott] and Johnnie [Flight-Lieutenant Johnston] and I had a consultation. Owing to the trouble of the gas we knew that our only chance was to leave on scheduled time. The weather forecast was not good, but we decided that we might cross the Channel and tie up at Le Bourget before the bad weather came. Scottie said, 'Now, look here, we are in for it, but for God's sake let's smile like damned Cheshire cats as we go on board and leave England with a clean pair of heels!'

Villiers: 'Could not Thomson have helped?'

Irwin: 'Oh dear. It's awful. You see, I told Thomson when he arrived at Cardington that gas had been escaping. Thomson said, "But this is negligible - and surely for this small matter you don't contemplate postponement? It's impossible. I am pledged to be back for the Imperial Conference. We must leave according to scheduled time!" I disagreed and consulted Scottie, but we decided to go. You know how late we were starting; and after crossing the Channel we three knew all was lost. We were desperate.'

Villiers: "Well, how exactly did the end come, and what was the cause? All evidence seems to show she dived, straightened, and dived again, and crashed.'

Irwin: Yes, that's so. Now I will tell you the truth: there was a tear in the cover. Now, listen very carefully. The wind was blowing hard and it was raining. Now you see what happened. The rush of the wind caused the first dive and then we straightened again. Another gust surging through this hole finished us.'

Major Villiers could not understand what had caused an explosion after the airship had actually hit the ground and the front underpart had been crushed.

Villiers: 'But, old boy, how could an engine cause the explosion?'

Irwin: 'It was this way. The diesel engine had been popping or back-firing[1] after crossing the Channel because the oil feed was not right. The oil is of too thick a consistency and has given some trouble before. You see the pressure in some of the gasbags was accentuated by the under-girders crumpling up and, since gas had been escaping, the extra pressure pushed the gas out with a rush, and at that moment the diesel engine back-fired and ignited the escaping gas. That caused the first explosion, and the others followed...'

On 2 November Major Villiers was present at a second seance and describes the control spirit as saying: 'I see near you a man of about fifty or fifty-five, jovial expression, hair growing a little grey by the ears. He used to have a moustache which made him look older. He now passes his hand across his lip and takes it away... He is smiling hard at you and says, "No, I won't give my name as I want to be certain you know who it is; very important." He is now putting his hand into his waistcoat pocket and is putting a piece of round glass into his eye, and says, "Now use your intelligence."'

Major Villiers says that it was not until this phrase was used that he recognized Sir Sefton Brancker's voice. Often when they were working together and disagreed on some point, Brancker would screw his monocle into his eye and exclaim testily, "Use your intelligence, use your damned intelligence!'

Villiers: 'Oh, Branks, old man! Of course it's you!... When did you first know or begin to realize that things on board were not right?'

Brancker: 'Well, we all had a conference because Irwin, Scottie, and Johnston put the case before us... Scott, Irwin and Johnston came and told T [Thomson]...of the gas trouble. The three, Scottie, Irwin and Johnston wanted to postpone flight, but Thomson said it's impossible, there has been so much talk and I have said so much and the GBP.'

Villiers: 'General who? I don't follow.'

Brancker: 'General British Public are all keyed up, we can't not go. They asked me and I felt I couldn't show a faint heart and, alas, said yes. We discussed the weather charts and saw that if we managed to cross the pond and could land somewhere in a foreign country, our honour would be vindicated and we could then bless the bad weather and say weather forced us to make a descent.'

Scottie: 'Oh, Villiers, it's all too ghastly for words, it's awful. Think of all the lives, experience and money, material - all thrown away and what for - for nothing.'

Villiers: 'Dear old man, there is a reason, even if we can't see it now.'

Scottie: That may be but it's absolutely ghastly'

Villiers: 'Now, dear Scottie, try and help me to fill in gaps. When did you begin to be suspicious that the ship was wrong?'

Scottie: 'After her first flight. She didn't handle too well and we had trouble.'

Villiers: 'Look here, can you explain what the gas valve trouble was? I have seen one of the actual valves in court.'

Scottie: The pressure of gas was too strong and gas was always forcing itself through. This was all wrong. But do you remember a gas valve was blown out and found away from the wreck?'

Villiers: 'Yes, I did hear this but how did it get blown off and not consumed in the flames?'

Scottie: 'It all really happened simultaneously. I will go on with the story of events and come on to that point again later.'

Villiers: 'All right, I quite agree.'

Scottie: 'Before we left we all had a conference and have calculated the amount of gas we were losing, we knew things were desperate.'

Villiers: "Yes, Brancker told me all that.'

Scottie: 'Surely, Villiers, old man, you, if faced with the awful position, would have done what we did. We had to uphold the honour of our country. What would Germany, USA and others have said if we had ratted? We *had* to go and take the 1000th chance of making a landing in France. We started off with that idea but being already late, were taken off our course and after crossing the water, we knew we had very little chance. It was hopeless to consider landing.'

Villiers: 'But since you had decided to try for Le Bourget, why did you not send out for a landing party?'

Scottie: 'We could not do so until after crossing the water, as if the message had been sent too early, we should have "blown the gaff and given the game away".'

Villiers: "Yes, I do realize you had to take all precautions to carry out the bluff. Who told you the news, and where were you?'

Scottie: "We - Johnnie, Irwin and I - were together.'

Villiers: 'In the control car?'

Scottie: 'No, Johnnie's cubbyhole, you know. The front rigger called to us and we saw by the instrument board immediately. We all gasped and were horrified at the news. We decided...'

Villiers (interrupting): 'Did she nosedive then?'

Scottie: 'No, not quite. We decided to make a turn and go with the wind as far as it was possible and make for Le Bourget and try at all costs some sort of landing. You know how we always turn a big circle because of the strain. So we decided to try. Well, Villiers, now imagine the picture. We have a bad rent in the cover on the starboard side. This brought about an unnatural pressure, and the frame gave a twist which, with the external pressure, forced us into our first dive. In the second, which was even worse, the pressure of the gasbags here was terrific and the gusts of wind were tremendous. This external pressure, coupled with the fact that the valve was weak, blew the valve right off and at the same time the released gas was ignited by a back-fire from the engine.'

On 21 November, Villiers told a voice which he believed was Sir Sefton Brancker's of his intentions about this matter. The more I think of it,' he said, 'the more I am convinced I must put all the information into JS'[2] hands.'

Brancker: 'Well done. I have been urging these fellows to...get the truth out at all costs.'

Villiers: 'I suppose the valves began to play up?'

Scottie: Yes, but more. The gas bags were not strong enough to hold the volume of gas, in other words were over-inflated, and when the bags were charged, each bag touched the other which caused a certain amount of friction and the skins became porous and so we had additional leakage, or evaporation. Remember the gas is not stationary but keeps moving round and round when set in motion, which happens in flight, and every time the ship came into a bump, condensation was caused. Added to this, our valves were weak.'

Villiers: 'Now, Scottie, I thought you said that just before the end you decided to turn and make for Le Bourget, but you were north and had not reached Paris.'

Scottie: 'What I said was, turning to try and land. On our way to Le Bourget. We heard the straining going on and sent the forward rigger to report. He came back and said the coupling had slipped, so we called two others and told them to try and make a new coupling by drilling new holes and bolting together, but of course there was no time. After that things happened quickly.'

Villiers: 'Now a thing that is puzzling the Court is how did Hunt know things were desperate since he had time to say "We're down, lads?" Did you tell him?'

Scottie: 'Well, all hands on duty in the ship knew the rent had been made and Hunt was actually off duty, but since he knew an hour before things were desperate, Hunt did what any other man would do and tried to give the warning to the men's quarters.'

Villiers: 'About what time did the rent appear?'

Scottie: 'I should say ten minutes to two - about ten minutes before the end came.'

Villiers: 'Was the first dive steep?'

Scottie: 'No. It was hardly a dive. You see, the rent had become bigger and the gusts of wind were hitting her hard, making her difficult to steer, and the girders were being badly strained. Our only chance was to try a slow turn and land downwind, which would enable the damaged starboard side to get shelter from the wind... We tried to correct the bump downwards, but she would not respond. Then she practically went into a perpendicular nosedive.'

Villiers: 'But evidence shows her nose did not strike the ground.'

Scottie: 'No, old boy, you're wrong. An aeroplane under those conditions would continue her nosedive, but since we had just commenced to try and turn, the gusts of wind blowing through the rent on her starboard put a terrific strain on her port side and she sort of got a drag on and heeled to port, thereby she finally landed on a more or less even keel. The rest you know.'

Villiers: 'Can you give me any approximate heights at different times? Try hard, old boy'

Scottie: 'I feel sure we never got over 900 or 950 feet and when we got over the channel, the wind and torrents of rain beat us down to possibly 250 to 300 feet. As we approached the French coast we seemed to catch a current that lifted us a bit but we never got much higher than 900, possibly that.'

Villiers: 'During that last 30 minutes, what height did you estimate?'

Scottie: 'Certainly not more than 900 feet. We never got to a proper satisfactory height.'

Villiers: 'I believe evidence was given that the order was given to shut off all engines. Why did you do this?'

Scottie: 'I will make this clear. We never did shut off all engines. Just as we contemplated turning, the order was given to slow down the forward port and starboard rear engines. This left us with the forward starboard and rear port and rear after engines running, which order was required to carry out the turn. But the turn was really hardly started when the final crash came. Remember it was the heel to port and the natural drag that put the ship in her final landing angle when she touched the ground, in fact, this practically operated like a brake.'

At a further seance, Villiers asked: 'Who was the front rigger who reported? I have brought a paper giving the list of those killed and will read you out the names of those killed, and you say Stop...Church.'

Scottie: 'Stop.'

Villiers: 'And who were the other two you told off to help Church? I will call down the list...Hastings.'

Scottie: 'Stop.'

Villiers: 'Oughton.'

Scottie: 'Stop...Hastings was on duty. Oughton was not, but we sent for him as he was the best man, and if he superintended the work we should have known it was OK...'

Later, Villiers asked the voice he believed to be Johnson's: 'Did you send out a message to Le Bourget?'

Johnston: 'No, we should have done, but of course the end came all too soon. We intended asking for a landing party of from three to four hundred men.'

Villiers: 'You admit then that from the moment she left the mooring mast, the behaviour of the ship was bad?'

Johnston: Yes, we all knew it and having to fly at those various heights was no child's play, believe me. But we had no choice.'

Villiers: 'Now what did you mean by, "Making up ballast?" '

Johnston: That meant we were changing over ballast'

Villiers: That meant dropping some.'

Johnston: 'Lord, no, we didn't drop any because we did not want to go up quickly or to any height because as I pointed out, the gas was churning round at a terrific rate. No, we simply changed her ballast from one tank to another to try and trim her to a better line.'

Villiers: 'Now, how were the weather reports before starting and how did they arrive?'

Johnston: 'I received charts at 2 pm and 4 pm and at 5.30 by W/T and again at about 6 by W/T. The 4 pm and 5.30 were not nice. Depression NNE wind SSW, and I knew when these met we should encounter dirty weather, and so we did. At 5.45 I called, or rather Irwin called, for ship's reports. Engine was not behaving. We had experienced trouble before. So even at this stage things were not pleasant. Then we started late. If we had started by 7 pm, I had then meant to hug the coastline, so as to try and get on the outer edge of the depression.'

So seriously did Major Villiers view all this information, and other facts that were communicated to him through the medium, that he approached the Air Ministry, and gave the substance of what had been said at the seances to the Under Secretary of State for Air. Further, he had known Sir John Simon, who was to preside over the Court of Inquiry into the disaster, since 1918, when Sir John was on Sir John Trenchard's staff and Villiers had been a senior intelligence officer. They had met several times since. Major Villiers therefore approached Sir John and they lunched together in a private room in the Law Courts and discussed the matter. Villiers felt very strongly that the statements made at the seances should be examined and that he should give evidence. He was not asked to do so.

1. In *The Aeroplane* of 8 October 1930, under the heading 'Some notes on the alterations in the R.101', L. Howard Flanders described the start from Cardington, and noted that 'the starboard forward engine was giving trouble... The main engine...exhaust...was a torrent of sparks which persisted for some minutes'.

Sir John Simon.

BIBLIOGRAPHY

Handbook on Rigid Airship No. 1, Parts I and II and Appendix, 1913, Admiralty, Air Dept., November 1913.

Handbook on HM Airship, Rigid, No. 9, Airship Dept., Admiralty, April 1918.

Commercial Airships, by H B Pratt, MINA (Chief Engineer, Airship Dept., Vickers Ltd.), Nelson, 1920.

Handbook on Rigid 23 Class Airships, Airship Dept., Admiralty, May 1918.

About Airships, by E F Spanner (E F Spanner), 1929.

The Tragedy of R.101, by E F Spanner (E F Spanner).

British Airships, Past, Present and Future, by George Whale. John Lane, The Bodley Head, 1929.

Zeppelin, The Story of a Great Achievement, 1922. Harry Vissering.

The Great Delusion - A Study of Aircraft in Peace and War, by 'Neon'. Ernest Benn, 1927.

Sefton Brancker, by Norman Macmillan. Heinemann, 1935.

Slide Rule, by Nevil Shute. House of Stratus, 2000.

Empire of the Air, by Lord Templewood (formerly Sir Samuel Hoare). Collins.

Retrospect, by Viscount Simon. Hutchinson, 1952.

Up Ship! by Lieut.-Commander C E Rosendahl. Dodd, Mead & Co., New York, 1931.

Airships in Peace and War, by Capt. J A Sinclair. Rich & Cowan, 1934.

The Story of the Airship (non-rigid), by Hugh Allen. Akron, Ohio, 1942.

The World, the Air and the Future, by Sir Dennistoun Burney (Knopf). 1929.

Encyclopaedia Britannica.

The London Magazine, 1784.

Diaries, logbooks, letters and private papers from many who worked on the construction of the airship, or who flew in her.

Registre de L'Etat Civil, 1930, and other records kept at the Mairie in Allonne (Oise), France.

The Report of the R.101 Inquiry, HMSO, 1931.

Files of *The Times, Daily Express, Daily Mail, Evening Standard, The Aeroplane, Flight, Illustrated London News, The Graphic,*

Sunday Pictorial, Bedfordshire Standard, Bedfordshire Record, Cardington Parish Magazine (November 1930), *The Evening News, The Sunday Graphic.*

Documents of the R. 101 Disaster Fund kept at the office of the Town Clerk of Bedford.

IF YOU ENJOYED THIS BOOK WHY NOT TRY SOME OTHER BOOKS BY JAMES LEASOR AND NOW AVAILABLE AS E-BOOKS:

FOLLOW THE DRUM

James Leasor's fictional tale, based on the events surrounding the Indian Mutiny.

India, in the mid-nineteenth century, was virtually run by a British commercial concern, the Honourable East India Company, whose directors would pay tribute to one Indian ruler and then depose another in their efforts to maintain their balance sheet of power and profit. But great changes were already casting shadows across the land, and when a stupid order was given to Indian troops to use cartridges greased with cow fat and pig lard (one animal sacred to the Hindus and the other abhorrent to Moslems) there was mutiny. The lives of millions were changed for ever including Arabella MacDonald, daughter of an English regular officer, and Richard Lang, an idealistic nineteen-year-old who began 1857 as a boy and ended it a man.

Pulling no punches, it shows up the good and the bad on both sides - the appalling stupidity and complacency of the British which caused the mutiny to happen, the chaos and venality of the insurgents, the ruthlessness of the retribution. It has everything, with a story based on the actual events.

MANDARIN-GOLD

The first of James Leasor's epic trilogy based on a Far Eastern trading company:

'Highly absorbing account of the corruption of an individual during a particularly sordid era of British imperial history,' *The Sunday Times*

'James Leasor switches to the China Sea more than a century ago, and with pace and ingenuity tells, in novel form, how the China coast was forced to open up its riches to Englishmen, in face of the Emperor's justified hostility' *Evening Standard*

'In the nasty story of opium - European and American traders made fortunes taking the forbidden dope into nineteenth century China, and this novel tells the story of their deadly arrangements and of the Emperor's vain attempts to stop them. Mr. Leasor has researched the

background carefully and the detail of the Emperor's lavish court but weak administration is fascinating. The white traders are equally interesting characters, especially those two real-life merchants, Jardine and Matheson.'
Manchester Evening News
It was the year of 1833 when Robert Gunn arrived on the China coast. Only the feeblest of defences now protected the vast and proud Chinese Empire from the ravenous greed of Western traders, and their opening wedge for conquest was the sale of forbidden opium to the native masses.

This was the path that Robert Gunn chose to follow... a path that led him through a maze of violence and intrigue, lust and treachery, to a height of power beyond most men's dreams — and to the ultimate depths of personal corruption.

Here is a magnificent novel of an age of plunder—and of a fearless freebooter who raped an empire.

THE CHINESE WIDOW
James Leasor's two preceding books in his chronicle of the Far East a century and half ago - FOLLOW THE DRUM and MANDARIN-GOLD were acclaimed by critics on both sides of the Atlantic. THE CHINESE WIDOW is their equal. It combines the ferocious force of the Dutch mercenaries who seek to destroy Gunn's plan; the pathos of a young woman left alone to rule a fierce and rebellious people; the gawky humour of Gunn's partner, the rough, raw Scot MacPherson; the mysterious yet efficacious practice of Chinese medicine, handed on through thousands of years...

When doctors in England pronounced his death sentence, Robert Gunn-founder of Mandarin-Gold, one of the most prosperous Far Eastern trading companies of the nineteenth century-vowed to spend his final year in creating a lasting memorial to leave behind him... to pay back, somehow, his debt to the lands of the East that had been the making of his vast fortune. He had a plan - a great plan - but to see it through he had to confront a fierce and rebellious people, a force of Dutch mercenaries and the Chinese Widow. Who was the Widow? What was her past-and her power...?

Action, suspense and the mysterious splendour of the Orient are combined in this exciting and moving novel.

BOARDING PARTY

Filmed as The Sea Wolves, this is the story of the undercover exploits of a territorial unit. The Germans had a secret transmitter on one of their ships in the neutral harbour of Goa. Its purpose was to guide the U-boats against Allied shipping in the Indian Ocean. There seemed no way for the British to infringe Goa's Portuguese neutrality by force. But the transmitter had to be silenced. Then it was remembered that 1,400 miles away in Calcutta was a source of possible help. A group of civilian bankers, merchants and solicitors were the remains of an old territorial unit called The Calcutta Light Horse. With a foreword by Earl Mountbatten of Burma.

'One of the most decisive actions in World War II was fought by fourteen out-of-condition middle-aged men sailing in a steam barge...' *Daily Mirror*

'Mr. Leasor's book is truth far more engrossing than fiction... A gem of World War II history' *New York Times*

'If ever there was a ready-made film script...here it is' *Oxford Mail*

GREEN BEACH

In 1942 radar expert Jack Nissenthall volunteered for a suicidal mission to join a combat team who were making a surprise landing at Dieppe in occupied France. His assignment was to penetrate a German radar station on a cliff above 'Green Beach: Because Nissenthall knew the secrets of British and US radar technology, he was awarded a personal bodyguard of sharpshooters. Their orders were to protect him, but in the event of possible capture to kill him. His choice was to succeed or die. The story of what happened to him and his bodyguards in nine hours under fire is one of World War II's most terrifying true stories of personal heroism.

'Green Beach has blown the lid off one of the Second World War's best-kept secrets' *Daily Express*

'If I had been aware of the orders given to the escort to shoot him rather than let him be captured, I would have cancelled them immediately' *Lord Mountbatten*

'Green Beach is a vivid, moving and at times nerve-racking reconstruction of an act of outstanding but horrific heroism' *Sunday Express*

THE RED FORT

James Leasor's gripping historical account of the Indian Mutiny.
'This is a battle piece of the finest kind, detailed, authentic and largely written from original documents. Mr. Leasor has a formidable gift of narrative. Never has this story of hate, violence, courage and cowardice been better told.'
Cecil Woodham-Smith in the *New York Times*

A year after the Crimean War ended, an uprising broke out in India which was to have equal impact on the balance of world power and the British Empire's role in world affairs. The revolt was against the East India Company which, not entirely against its will, had assumed responsibility for administering large parts of India. The ostensible cause of the mutiny sprang from a rumour that cartridges used by the native Sepoy troops were greased with cow's fat and pig's lard — cows being sacred to the Hindus, and pigs abhorred by the Mohammedans. But the roots of the trouble lay far deeper, and a bloody and ineptly handled war ensued.

The Red Fort is a breath-taking account of the struggle, with all its cruelties, blunderings and heroic courage. When peace was finally restored, the India we know today began to emerge.

THE MARINE FROM MANDALAY
This is the true story of a Royal Marine wounded by shrapnel in Mandalay in WW2 who undergoes a long solitary march to the Japanese through the whole of Burma and then finds his way back through India and back to Britain to report for duty in Plymouth. On his way he has many encounters and adventures and helps British and Indian refugees. He also has to overcome complete disbelief that a single man could walk out of Burma with nothing but his orders - to report to HQ - and his initiative.

THE MILLIONTH CHANCE
The R101 airship was thought to be the model for the future, an amazing design that was 'as safe as houses ... except for the millionth chance'. On the night of 4 October 1930 that chance in a million came up, however. James Leasor brilliantly reconstructs the conception and crash of this huge ship of the air with compassion for the forty-seven dead - and only six survivors.

'The sense of fatality grows with every page ... Gripping' *Evening Standard*

THE ONE THAT GOT AWAY
Franz von Werra was a Luftwaffe pilot shot down in the Battle of Britain. The One that Got Away tells the full and exciting story of his two daring escapes in England and his third and successful escape: a leap from the window of a prisoners' train in Canada. Enduring snow and frostbite, he crossed into the then neutral United States. Leasor's book is based on von Werra's own dictated account of his adventures and makes for a compelling read.
'A good story, crisply told' *New York Times*

THE PLAGUE AND THE FIRE
This dramatic story chronicles the horror and human suffering of two terrible years in London's history. 1665 brought the plague and cries of 'Bring Out Your Dead' echoed through the city. A year later, the already decimated capital was reduced to ashes in four days by the fire that began in Pudding Lane. James Leasor weaves in the first-hand accounts of Daniel Defoe and Samuel Pepys, among others.
'An engrossing and vivid impression of those terrible days' *Evening Standard*
'Absorbing ... an excellent account of the two most fantastic years in London's history' *Sunday Express*

WHO KILLED SIR HARRY OAKES?
James Leasor cleverly reconstructs events surrounding a brutal and unusual murder. It is 1943 and Sir Harry Oakes lies horrifically murdered at his Bahamian mansion. Although a self-made multi-millionaire, Sir Harry is an unlikely victim - there are no suggestions of jealousy or passion. Leasor makes the daring suggestion that Sir Harry Oakes' murder, the burning of the liner Normandie in New York Harbour in 1942 and the Allied landings in Sicily are all somehow connected.

'The story has all the right ingredients - rich occupants of a West Indian tax haven, corruption, drugs, the Mafia, and a weak character as governor' *Daily Mail*

PASSPORT TO OBLIVION

Passport to Oblivion is the first case book of Dr. Jason Love . . . country doctor turned secret agent. Multi-million selling, published in 19 languages around the world and filmed as Where the Spies Are starring David Niven.

'As K pushed his way through the glass doors of the Park Hotel, he realized instinctively why the two stumpy men were waiting by the reception desk. They had come to kill him. ...'

Who was K - and why should anyone kill him? Who was the bruised girl in Rome? Why did a refugee strangle his mistress in an hotel on the edge of the Arctic Circle? And why, in a small office above a wholesale fruiterers in Covent Garden, did a red-haired Scot sift through filing cabinets for the name of a man he knew in Burma twenty years ago?

None of these questions might seem to concern Dr Jason Love, a country practitioner of Bishop's Combe, Somerset. But, in the end, they all do. Apart from his patients, Dr Love has apparently only two outside interests: his supercharged Cord roadster, and the occasional Judo lessons he gives to the local branch of the British Legion.

But out of the past, to which all forgotten things should belong, a man comes to see him - and his simple, everyday country-life world is shattered like a mirror by a .38 bullet.

"Heir Apparent to the golden throne of Bond" *The Sunday Times*

PASSPORT TO PERIL

Passport to Peril is Dr Jason Love's second brilliant case history in suspense. An adventure that sweeps from the gentle snows of Switzerland to the freezing peaks of the Himalayas, and ends in a blizzard of violence, hate, and lust on the roof of the world. Guns, girls and gadgets all play there part as the Somerset doctor, old car expert and amateur secret agent uncovers a mystery involving the Chinese intelligence service and a global blackmail ring.

"Second instalment in the exploits of Dr Jason Love... Technicolour backgrounds, considerable expertise about weapons... action, driven along with terrific vigour" *The Sunday Times*

"It whips along at a furious pace" *The Sun*

"A great success" *The Daily Express*

PASSPORT IN SUSPENSE

'A superb example of thriller writing at its best' *Sunday Express*
'Third of Dr Love's supercharged adventures... It starts in the sunshine of the Bahamas, swings rapidly by way of a brunette corpse into Mexico, and winds up in the yacht of a megalomaniac ex-Nazi... Action: non-stop: Tension: nail-biting' *Daily Express*
'His ingenuity and daring are as marked as ever' *Birmingham Post*
When a German submarine mysteriously disappears on a NATO exercise in the North Sea, and a beautiful girl was brutally murdered in the Bahamas, there at first seemed little connection between the two events. But the missing sub was a vital link in a deadly plan to conquer the West, master-minded by a megalomaniac ex-Nazi. And the dead girl was an Israeli agent intent on bringing to trial the ex-Nazis hiding in South America.
Dr Jason Love, the Somerset GP–turned part-time British secret agent, was enjoying a quiet holiday in Nassau, on his way to an old car rally in Mexico, when he witnessed the girl's murder. Before he knew it, he found himself dragged into the affair. He duly travels to Mexico, thinking he has left this behind, but becomes plunged into a violent situation, with his life in danger – and a desperate mission to foil a terrifying plot to destroy Western civilisation as we know it…

THEY DON'T MAKE THEM LIKE THAT ANY MORE
It introduces the randy, earthy and likeable proprietor of Aristo Autos who deals in vintage cars - not forgetting Sara, supercharged with sexual promise, who whets his curiosity and rouses his interest.
In the process of becoming a reluctant hero, he spins across France, Spain and Switzerland, on the track of a rare Mercedes too badly wanted by too many dangerous men. . .
'Devoured at a sitting. . . racy, pungent and swift' *The Sunday Times*
'Number one thriller on my list ...sexy and racy' *Sunday Mirror*
'A racy tale . . . the hero spends most of his time trying to get into beds and out of trouble . . . plenty of action, anecdotes, and inside dope on exotic old cars' *Sunday Express*

NEVER HAD A SPANNER ON HER
In the sequel to "They Don't Make Them Like That Any More" our vintage car dealer gets involved in a scheme to import some vintage cars from Nasser's Egypt. From the run of the mill trades of London our hero finds himself in Cairo and trying to export a Bugatti

Royale, probably the rarest car on the planet. The story has suspense, guns, a beautiful girl and of course masses of old cars. It races from Belgravia, to Belsize Park to the Pyramids and Alexandria. Leasor combines his proven thriller writing skills with an encyclopaedic knowledge of vintage cars to deliver a real page turner.

`Mr. Leasor has a delightful sense of the ridiculous; he also has an educated style which stems from more than 20 very good books.'   *Manchester Evening News*

`All good reading, with accurate detail of the cars involved.' *Autocar*

`Vintage adventure for auto-lovers and others alike.' *The Evening News*

HOST OF EXTRAS

The bawdy, wise-cracking owner of Aristo Autos is offered two immaculate vintage Rolls straight out of a collector's dream: one is a tourer, the other an Alpine. The cars, and Aristo, get in on a shady film deal which leads to a trip to Corsica with the imperturbable Dr Jason Love - Somerset GP and part-time secret agent - his supercharged Cord and the infinitely desirable Victoria – and to the cut and thrust of violent international skulduggery.

"An entertaining and fast moving adventure" *Daily Express*

'It's all great fun and games, with plenty of revs.' *Evening Standard*

'. . . a clutch of thrills and sparks of wit.' *The Yorkshire Post*

James Leasor was educated at The City of London School and Oriel College, Oxford. In World War II he was commissioned into the Royal Berkshire Regiment and posted to the 1st Lincolns in Burma and India, where he served for three and a half years. His experiences there stimulated his interest in India, both past and present, and inspired him to write such books as Boarding Party (filmed as The Sea Wolves), The Red Fort, Follow the Drum and NTR. He later became a feature writer and foreign correspondent at the Daily Express. There he wrote The One that Got Away, the story of the sole German POW to escape from Allied hands. As well as non-fiction, Leasor has written novels, including the Dr Jason Love series, which have been published in 19 countries. Passport to Oblivion was filmed as Where the Spies Are with David Niven. He died in September 2007.

James Leasor's books are becoming available as ebooks. Please visit www.jamesleasor.com for details on all these books or contact info@jamesleasor.com for more information on availability. Follow on Twitter: @jamesleasor for details on new releases.

Jason Love novels
Passport to Oblivion (filmed, and republished in paperback, as Where the Spies Are)
Passport to Peril (Published in the U.S. as Spylight)
Passport in Suspense (Published in the U.S. as The Yang Meridian)
Passport for a Pilgrim
A Week of Love
Love-all
Love and the Land Beyond
Frozen Assets
Love Down Under

Jason Love and Aristo Autos novel
Host of Extras

Aristo Autos novels
They Don't Make Them Like That Any More
Never Had A Spanner On Her

Robert Gunn novels
Mandarin-Gold
The Chinese Widow
Jade Gate

Other novels
Not Such a Bad Day
The Strong Delusion
NTR: Nothing to Report
Follow the Drum
Ship of Gold
Tank of Serpents

Non-fiction

The Monday Story
Author by Profession
Wheels to Fortune
The Serjeant-Major; a biography of R.S.M. Ronald Brittain, M.B.E., Coldstream Guards
The Red Fort
The One That Got Away
The Millionth Chance: The Story of The R.101
War at the Top (published in the U.S. as The Clock With Four Hands)
Conspiracy of Silence
The Plague and the Fire
Rudolf Hess: The Uninvited Envoy
Singapore: the Battle that Changed the World
Green Beach
Boarding Party (filmed, and republished in paperback, as The Sea Wolves)
The Unknown Warrior (republished in paperback as X-Troop)
The Marine from Mandalay
Rhodes & Barnato: the Premier and the Prancer

As Andrew MacAllan (novels)
Succession
Generation
Diamond Hard
Fanfare
Speculator
Traders

As Max Halstock
Rats – The Story of a Dog Soldier

www.jamesleasor.com

Follow on Twitter: @jamesleasor

16153362R00104

Printed in Great Britain
by Amazon